Haynes

Build your own
Website

Published by: Haynes Publishing
Sparkford, Yeovil, Somerset BA22 7JJ, UK
Tel: 01963 442030 Fax: 01963 440001
Int. tel: +44 1963 442030 Fax: +44 1963 440001
E-mail: sales@haynes.co.uk
Website: www.haynes.co.uk

British Library Cataloguing in Publication Data:
A catalogue record for this book is available from the British Library

ISBN 1 84425 116 0

Printed in Britain by J. H. Haynes & Co. Ltd., Sparkford

Throughout this book, trademarked names are used. Rather than put a
trademark symbol after every occurrence of a trademarked name, we use
the names in an editorial fashion only, and to the benefit of the trademark
owner, with no intention of infringement of the trademark. Where such
designations appear in this book, they have been printed with initial caps.

Whilst we at J. H. Haynes & Co. Ltd. strive to ensure the accuracy and
completeness of the information in this book, it is provided entirely at the
risk of the user. Neither the company nor the author can accept liability
for any errors, omissions or damage resulting therefrom. In particular,
users should be aware that component and accessory manufacturers, and
software providers, can change specifications without notice, thus
appropriate professional advice should always be sought.

Haynes

Build your own
Website

Kyle MacRae

Contents

Introduction

Getting a personal foothold on the World Wide Web is not difficult. It used to be, certainly, but times have changed. These days, it's perfectly possible for anybody to publish a single web page, a joined-up website or a funky blog with virtually no previous experience and for minimal (or zero) expense. The learning curve is shallow and the rewards are immediate. Above all, it's great fun.

There are as many reasons for making websites as there are pages on the internet, ranging from the worthy to the wacky. Some people photograph their cats and publish the pictures for the world to see, while others use their websites as public diaries to keep in touch with friends. Families with faraway relatives use their sites to let aunts in Australia see the toddlers' latest antics, and victims of chronic pain or serious illnesses use their sites to share their experiences with fellow sufferers and to provide support to one another.

With 8,058,044,651 pages to choose from (at the last count, one minute ago), you'll never be short of something to read – but reading is only the beginning.

You're the voice

What makes the internet so amazing is that you're not limited to reading other people's work. You can join in the conversation. So, for example, if you think newspaper coverage of your pet subject is patchy or plain wrong, you can create your own rival publication in seconds without spending a single penny. You could set up a discussion forum dedicated to a specific subject – politics, local events, shoes, cute things cats do – and get chatting with like-minded souls from the other side of the planet. You could take photographs of strange places in your home town and publish them for the world to see, or you could build a site about the joy of sheds. The only limit is your own imagination.

Your site could be:

- An electronic magazine where you're the editor, the publisher and the star reporter
- A photo gallery that lets far-flung relatives see your snaps
- A place for you to let off steam about the things that annoy you
- A place to show off your skills, interests or strange party tricks
- A comprehensive library of information about a subject you hold dear
- A forum where like-minded souls can get together, chat and share their top tips
- An online shop selling things you've made, or things you're an expert on

…or anything else you can think of.

Options for all

There are several ways to acquire a presence on the internet and we cover three main approaches in this book:

- Designing a "traditional" page or site with WYSIWYG (what you see is what you get) software. This is as easy as writing a letter in a word processor or, perhaps more accurately, designing a leaflet with a desktop-publishing program. Grab a little free web space – we'll show you how – and you can be live and online in minutes.
- Publishing a weblog, or blog. Blogs used to be thought of as online diaries but there's much, much more to blogging than that. We'll take you through the basics and beyond.
- Building a site by hand. Yes, it sounds daunting but HTML – the language of the web – is logical and straightforward. You can easily create a page by hand using nothing more complicated, or expensive, than a free text editor program. Even if you decide to go down the WYSIWYG or blogging route, a little HTML knowledge is invaluable when it comes to understanding what's going on behind the scenes.

We also go through the processes of registering a domain name and buying web space, and we glance at the dark art of search engine optimisation and the possibility of setting up an online shop.

Designing a website and seeing it go live on the internet is a tremendously rewarding project, whether you do so just for the fun of it or with serious purpose in mind.

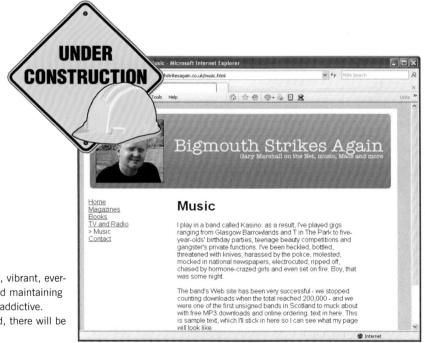

A website is a living, vibrant, ever-changing thing - and maintaining your own is utterly addictive. Once you get started, there will be no stopping you.

1

PART **1**

So you want to build a website?

PART ❶ Let's get started

If you can imagine it, there's a site on the internet dedicated to it. Anti-bullying? There's the Anti-Bullying Network at **www.antibullying.net**. Food? Take your pick from Delia Smith (**www.deliaonline.com**), Jamie Oliver (**www.jamieoliver.com**) or sites such as BBC Food (**www.bbc.co.uk/food**). Famous quotations? Brainy Quote (**www.brainyquote.com**). The effectiveness of different forms of medical treatment? Try **www.clinicalevidence.com**. The best articles from the world's literary journals? Arts & Letters Daily (**www.aldaily.com**). So what's your site going to be about?

Well, before you decide on the content or the look of your own site, it's a very good idea to have a look at the best and the worst sites on the World Wide Web. Some sites are spectacular, amazing electronic emporiums that make the world a better, happier or smarter place; and others are a complete waste of time and electricity.

The good: Feed Me Better (www.feedmebetter.com)
The Feed Me Better site was designed to support celebrity chef Jamie Oliver's campaign for healthier school dinners, and it was a roaring success. The site attracted 271,677 signatures for its online petition, embarrassed the government into taking action and helped thousands of parents find out more about the importance of decent school dinners.

Jamie Oliver's campaign for better school meals was a big success, and the Feed Me Better website played a crucial part in putting pressure on the government.

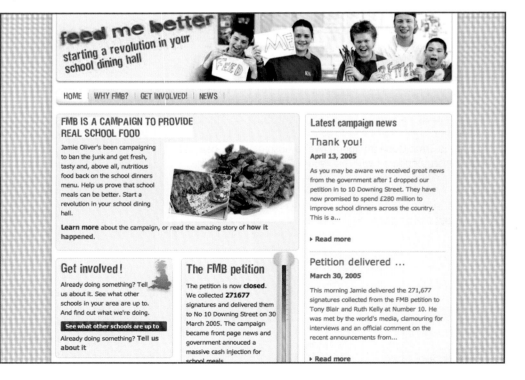

feed me better
starting a revolution in your school dining hall

HOME | WHY FMB? | GET INVOLVED! | NEWS

FMB IS A CAMPAIGN TO PROVIDE REAL SCHOOL FOOD

Jamie Oliver's been campaigning to ban the junk and get fresh, tasty and, above all, nutritious food back on the school dinners menu. Help us prove that school meals can be better. Start a revolution in your school dining hall.

Learn more about the campaign, or read the amazing story of **how it happened**.

Get involved!
Already doing something? Tell us about it. See what other schools in your area are up to. And find out what we're doing.

See what other schools are up to

Already doing something? **Tell us about it**

The FMB petition
The petition is now **closed**. We collected **271677** signatures and delivered them to No 10 Downing Street on 30 March 2005. The campaign became front page news and government annouced a massive cash injection for school meals

Latest campaign news

Thank you!
April 13, 2005
As you may be aware we received great news from the government after I dropped our petition in to 10 Downing Street. They have now promised to spend £280 million to improve school dinners across the country. This is a...

▸ **Read more**

Petition delivered ...
March 30, 2005
This morning Jamie delivered the 271,677 signatures collected from the FMB petition to Tony Blair and Ruth Kelly at Number 10. He was met by the world's media, clamouring for interviews and an official comment on the recent announcements from...

▸ **Read more**

The site itself is a great bit of web design. It's clean and uncluttered, it's easy to find your way around, and the images and colour scheme have been carefully chosen to make each page as friendly and as inviting as possible. Despite being packed with information – news, nutrition information, details of various schools' activities – it isn't intimidating; and while the site is ultimately a commercial one (there are plenty of opportunities to buy Jamie Oliver books and DVDs), it managed to achieve something worthwhile: better food for kids.

The bad: Wow Banking (www.wowbanking.com)

Oh dear, oh dear, oh dear. This site might look like a spoof, but it isn't: it's a real bank's site, and it's a classic example of how not to design a website. The colours are awful (and sore on the eyes), the layout is appalling, the front page includes horrible animated images and a nauseating, pulsing logo, and much of the text is unreadable. White text on a lime green background? Eek!

The site isn't just bad from a design point of view, though. It could be bad from a business point of view, too. Banking is a serious matter, and you might not entrust your savings and investments to any firm whose site seems to have been put together by toddlers.

A badly designed site isn't good for business.

The ugly: Time Cube (www.timecube.com)

Time Cube is quite an achievement: not only is it completely incomprehensible, but it's also horrible to look at. Text is underlined in random places before BURSTING INTO CAPITALS or appearing in retina-burning colours. If you spend more than two seconds looking at it you'll develop a migraine, so chances are you won't.

So what is Time Cube all about? We've absolutely no idea. It's utter gibberish, peppered with big words and laced with the occasional profanity. Here's one of the more accessible sentences: "Time Cube proves a 1 face god impossible, due to 4 corner face metamorphic human – baby, child and grandparent faces." If that makes sense to you, seek help immediately.

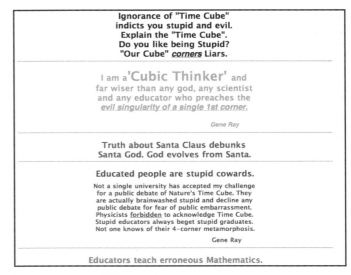

We've no idea what this chap is on about, and the headache-inducing design means we won't be hanging around to find out.

Amazon.co.uk is an amazingly successful online shop, and it owes a big part of its success to usability. It's a winning design that's been widely imitated by other online shops.

How to win friends and influence people

There are lots of really bad sites on the internet, but very few of them are intentionally bad. In many cases, the site owners forgot the Golden Rule of websites: put yourself in your visitors' shoes.

When you're putting your pages together, you need to think about usability and accessibility.

Usability is really just common sense. Is it easy to see which bits of a page are supposed to be clicked? Is the text readable? Is the layout sensible? Generally if a site looks like an explosion in a paint factory, if it's horribly cluttered and if it's impossible to work out what's going on, then the site owner hasn't thought about usability.

The best way to learn about usability is to look at a site that gets it right, such as Amazon.co.uk. It's one of the world's favourite shops, and much of its success is due to its simple, effective and very usable design. There's a big logo at the top left of the screen, and no matter where you are in the site you can click on that logo to return to the front page. Links to different bits of the site – books, DVDs, electronics and so on – are shown as tabs along the top of the screen, and it's always obvious what you need to click and what each bit of the page does.

A great deal of thought has gone into the design of Amazon.co.uk, and you'll find that most online shops look very, very similar. That's not an accident: it's a winning design, and customers now expect online shops to look and feel like Amazon. However, usability isn't limited to online shops. For example, Google is packed with powerful tools but the front page is clean, simple and effective, which means it's eminently usable. The same applies to the BBC site, or the *Guardian* newspaper site.

If a site isn't usable, it's unlikely to become successful.

Access for everyone

Usability and accessibility go together like love and marriage: if a site isn't usable, it's unlikely to be accessible either. Accessibility is incredibly important – in fact, if your site is a business one then you can be fined if it isn't accessible.

To make a site accessible, you need to think of two kinds of visitors. You need to consider the needs of people with disabilities such as partial blindness, and you need to consider the needs of people who might not have the same hardware and software as you.

The internet is a fantastic resource for people with disabilities, but thoughtless website design often puts obstacles in their way. For example, blind people can use special software called a screen reader to browse websites, but if a site designer puts all of the site's text into graphics files then the screen reader won't be able to read out those sections. There is a way around this – every well-known website design program enables you to use special tags that describe images to screen reader software – but many designers don't use those tags. Recognising this, the RNIB has put together a fantastic collection of articles about accessible websites at **www.rnib.co.uk**.

If you're running a site for business then an accessible site is a legal requirement. The Disability Discrimination Act makes it an offence for businesses to discriminate against people with disabilities, and inaccessible websites do just that. However, it's important to think about accessibility whether you're running an online shop or a daft diary. The whole point of publishing on the internet is for your site to be available to others, and an inaccessible site simply locks out a portion of your potential audience.

The wrong trousers

Imagine if Marks & Spencer wouldn't let you in unless your shoes were a very specific shade of brown, or if HMV banned any customer with black hair. Crazy? Of course it is – but a similar thing happens online every day.

Many site owners forget that not everyone in the world uses the same kit as they do. For example, you might have a PC running Internet Explorer, but some of your visitors might have an Apple Mac running the Safari browser. Until recently some big-name sites – Direct Line Insurance and Marks & Spencer, for example – wouldn't let Safari users enter their sites. Instead, a fancy bit of site design detected that they weren't using Internet Explorer and displayed a big No Entry sign. Others simply didn't work properly. If you attempted to view the Odeon Cinemas website using the Firefox or Safari browsers, you'd get a blank screen. Essentially these sites were saying to visitors, "Go away! We don't want your money!"

It's not just your web browser, though. Some people browse the web using "smart" mobile phones, or Pocket PCs, or PlayStation Portables. Some people have PCs with teeny-weeny screens, while others have monitors that are bigger than most people's TVs. Some people have one monitor on their desk, while others have two. Some people like to use high resolution displays, while others prefer nice big type. Some people browse with images turned off, while others like to see the pretty pictures. Some people have amazingly fast internet connections, while others are halfway up a hill trying to get a connection with their mobile phone.

The only thing these various people have in common is that their systems, software or setup are different to yours. The good news is that it's really easy to make sure that your site will work on any bit of kit, on any web browser and on anybody's choice of machine. We'll show you how to do just that in a later chapter.

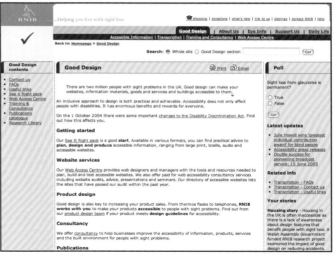

The RNIB has put together an excellent collection of resources that explains why accessibility is so important and shows you how to get it right.

This is what the Odeon Cinemas website looks like in the Firefox browser, which is used by 10% of internet browsers. The Odeon is missing out on an awful lot of business.

PART 1

Nuts and bolts

Building a website is very, very easy. The World Wide Web is much simpler than you might expect, and once you understand the nuts and bolts of how websites work you'll find it easy to create a website with the "wow!" factor.

To create a website you need three things: the pages that make up the site itself, a place to put those pages, and a way to make the pages available to anyone on the internet. We'll find out how to create pages throughout this book, but before we can start creating we need to explain a few bits of jargon.

How web pages work

What makes a web page different from a normal document is the hyperlink, or link for short. Links are the bits of web pages that do something such as open another page, play a sound clip or take you to another site altogether. You'll see them on almost every page of the web. These links create a giant web of information spread across the globe, which is why the phrase World Wide Web was coined to describe it.

A web page is simply a text file that sits on a computer and contains a list of instructions. It's a bit like driving directions but instead of telling your visitors to turn left at the traffic lights, it tells your visitors' web browsing software what to show on screen, what links to include in the page and, crucially, what to do when someone clicks on one of those links.

When you look at a link, what you see on screen isn't the same thing your browser sees. For example, you might see the following text underlined in blue:

Click here to see photos of my cat!

But your browser will see something like this:

http://www.siteaboutmycats.co.uk/photos.htm

The http:// bit tells your web browser that, when you click on the link, it should load another file (http stands for HyperText Transfer Protocol, which is worth knowing if you frequent pub quizzes; otherwise you can forget about it again) and the bit after the two slashes is the actual address of that page.

Internet addresses look a bit complicated, but they're straightforward enough when you know what each bit means. In our example, the "www" means that the site is on the World Wide Web, and "siteaboutmycats.co.uk" is the name of the website. The last bit of the address is the name of the file. In this case, it's a web page called "photos.htm".

The link gives your web browser the electronic equivalent of driving directions. In our example the link says: "Go onto the internet, look on the World Wide Web for siteaboutmycats.co.uk, and then load the file called photos.htm".

Web addresses can also include folders, just like on your

Google offers new stock at $295
BBC News, UK - 43 minutes ago
Google says it will price its latest stock sale at $295 (£162.55) a share, more than three times the price of its initial public offering last year. ...
Calif. judge to consider throwing out **Google** suit CNET News.com
Google Wins Microsoft Case The Moscow Times
Judge's compromise ruling on **Google**-Microsoft case Financial Mirror
ZDNet UK - Wired News - all 386 related »

Washington Post

Google boosts blogging
News24, South Africa - hours ago
San Francisco - A new **Google** speciality search engine sifts through the internet's millions of frequently updated personal journals, a long-anticipated ...
Google Launches Tool to Search for Blog Updates Los Angeles Times
Google Offering Raises $4.18B Red Herring
Google Launches Search Engine For Blogs InformationWeek
Washington Post - Boston Herald - all 152 related »

Pocket-lint.co.uk

Google looking to get 4.4B richer
New York Daily News, NY - 1 hour ago
Google, the most-used Internet search engine, was expected to raise $4.41 billion yesterday in its first stock sale since going public, the largest such ...
Google prices stock offering at $295 per share Hindustan Times
Google stock offering at $295 per share Rediff
Google May Expand in China, Buy More Computers With Sale Funds Bloomberg
Bloomberg - Malaysia Star - all 82 related »

Google swaps hippy talk for happy talk

Web pages are full of links, usually – but not always – underlined and blue.

computer. So for example you could have addresses such as these:

http://www.siteaboutmycats.co.uk/oldstuff/photos.htm

This time, once the browser has found the "siteaboutmycats.co.uk" site, it needs to look in the folder "oldstuff" for the appropriate file. Or you might have:

http://www.siteaboutmycats.co.uk/oldstuff/archive/2004/ photos.htm

Once again the browser heads for "siteaboutmycats.co.uk" but this time the link tells it to open the "oldstuff" folder, then the "archive" folder, then the "2004" folder.

It's almost identical to the way your computer works. For example, you might save a document in your My Documents folder, and it would have the following address:

C:\My Documents\myfile.doc

Or you might have folders within the My Documents folder, such as:

C:\My Documents\house stuff\myfile.doc
C:\My Documents\daft stuff\cartoon.jpg
C:\My Documents\accounts\2005\nasty letter to the bank.doc

For reasons too dull to explain, the slashes in your web browser rise from left to right when you view files and folders, but when you're looking at folders on your computer in Windows the slashes fall from left to right.

Each file on your computer has an "address", just like every page on the internet.

So, we know how web addresses work – but you can't have an address if your pages aren't on the internet in the first place. To do that, we'll need to explore the world of web space.

Are you being served?

Every website needs to be stored on something called a web server, which is a fancy way of saying "computer". A web server is simply a computer with a bit of hard disk space and a permanent internet connection, and it's configured in such a way that it can dish out web pages whenever your visitors request them.

Although it's possible to run your own web server, it's a much better idea to let someone else do it on your behalf. That means you don't need to worry about setting up the server, mucking around with advanced configuration options and ensuring that it has a permanent internet connection.

Firms who provide space for web pages are known as hosting firms, because they host your website on your behalf. There are hundreds of such firms to choose from, and they offer a huge range of packages ranging from free and easy services for internet beginners to massive systems for giant online shops.

Firms such as Tripod can give you everything you need to publish your website, and their most basic package is free of charge.

To pay or not to pay

Web hosting comes in two flavours: free hosting, which enables you to publish a site without paying a penny, and paid hosting, which costs money.

Free hosting is available from firms such as Tripod (**www.tripod.co.uk**) and is designed to be beginner-friendly. You'll get enough space for a decent collection of pages, a few tools to help you improve your site such as free guestbook software, free images or other goodies, and signing up only takes a few seconds. However, there is a trade-off. Most such services will add advertising banners or pop-up windows to your pages, and you'll find that few free hosts will let you store video clips, music files or other hefty downloads.

Paid hosting costs money, but it's much more flexible. Firms such as Pipex (**www.pipex.net**) and 1&1 (**www.oneandone.co.uk**) offer packages starting at just £4.99 per month, and they won't add any advertising to your site. Depending on the specific package you choose you'll usually be able to store video clips, music files and other big files, and you'll get much more space and much more scope than with a free host.

So which should you choose? The table below shows the key differences between a typical free hosting service and one that costs money.

Before you make the decision, though, it's a very good idea to see if your Internet Service Provider gives you any web space as part of your internet connection package. Many ISPs do, and it's a good compromise between the two kinds of hosting: the space comes free with your internet service but it won't spoil your pages by plastering adverts all over the place.

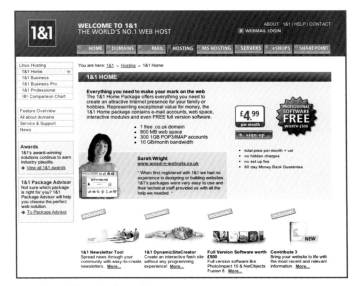

Paid-for web hosting is much more flexible than free hosting and prices aren't too scary: 1&1's home package starts at £4.99 per month.

	Typical free host	Typical paid host
How much will I pay?	Nothing	From £4.99 per month
Will the firm add adverts?	Yes	No
How much web space will I get?	Not much	Lots
Can I get more space if I need it?	For a fee	For a fee
Can I use photos?	Yes	Yes
Can I use video?	Probably not	Yes
Can I use sound files?	Probably not	Yes
Is it easy to set up?	Very	Fairly
What happens if I get too many visitors?	Site may be temporarily unavailable	You may incur extra charges,but only after attracting serious visitor numbers
Can I sell ad space on my site?	Depends on the hosting firm	Yes
Can I run an online shop?	Not usually	Yes
Can I install extra features?	Only host-approved ones	Yes, anything you like
Will I get technical support?	Not usually	Yes
Will the firm take backups of my site?	Not usually	Yes
Who is it best for?	Beginners, very simple sites	Everyone

What's in a name?

No matter what kind of hosting you go for, the address of your website is likely to be rather complicated. In most cases, you'll end up with something like this:

www.hostingfirm.com/hosting/users/g535433/index.html

You can change this by getting your own domain name. Domain names are the addresses of internet sites such as Amazon.co.uk, Google.com, BBC.co.uk and so on, and you can pick up one of your very own for around £3 from a site such as 123Reg (**www.123reg.co.uk**). Once you've bought the name, it's yours for two years and you can point it to your website through the 123Reg control panel. That means your site can have a snappier name such as "mygreatsite.co.uk" instead of the random-looking address you get with your web space.

There are several good reasons for buying a domain name. First, it's easier to remember. Secondly, it makes your site more search-friendly. Search engines give weight to a site's domain name, so if two sites have identical content but one is called **interestingthings.com** and the other is **hostingfirm.com/space/2005/users/jim/home**, then the snappier name will appear higher in search results for the phrase "interesting things".

The third reason to get a domain name is that it's portable, so if you're currently using a free web host and decide to move to paid hosting, you can simply point the domain name to your site's new location. Similarly if you decide that your current paid host isn't up to the job and you want to move to a competitor, you can do so without any disruption whatsoever.

Before you buy a domain name it's worth looking at the different options. While **.com** domains are the most desirable, they cost £30+ to register; **.org.uk** domains should only be used by non-profit organisations; **.ltd.uk** domains are for UK Limited Companies; and gimmicky domains such as **.me** and **.biz** are rather naff. The best all-rounder is the **.co.uk** domain, which is very popular and very cheap.

Once you've chosen the kind of domain name you want, you also need to choose the name itself. This can be a bit of a minefield, for two reasons: many of the obvious names have already been sold, and you also need to make sure you don't upset anyone with more money than you. For example, "markzandspencer.co.uk" might still be available to buy, but if you use it you can expect an unfriendly letter from Marks & Spencer's crack legal team. If any firm thinks you're trying to attract visitors that are rightfully theirs, expect legal hot water.

Don't bother with generic terms such as "food", "shopping", "news", "computers" and so on: you can be sure they've been snapped up already (for instance, **www.food.co.uk** takes you to a shopping directory). Most common surnames have been taken, as have common first name/surname combinations. That's why there are so many internet companies with weird names: they racked their brains until they came up with a domain name that was available, and when they came up with one they named the company after it. You might find that you need to do a bit of lateral thinking to come up with a suitably snappy domain name that hasn't already been snapped up by somebody else.

You can buy a snappy domain name such as "mygreatsite.co.uk" for around £3 per year.

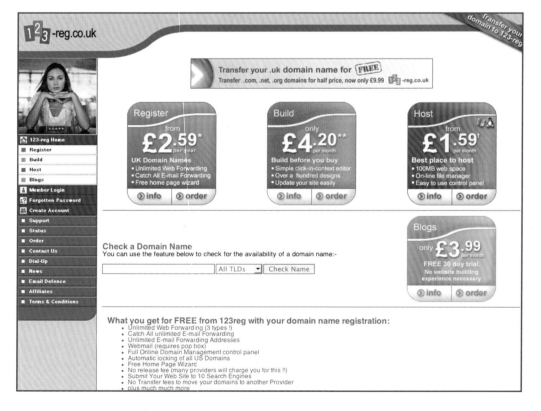

Buying a domain name and hosting

Now that we've discovered the importance of domain names and web space, the next step is to buy them both. If you've already got free web space from your ISP or from a free hosting provider, then you might want to experiment with that before spending any money. However, if you want your site to look the business then a decent domain name and professional, ad-free web space will be a big help.

1

*Web hosting is fiercely competitive, so it pays to shop around. At the time of writing, 123reg (**www.123reg.co.uk**) was offering one of the best deals around, with an entry-level hosting package for just £1.59 per month. Click on the Host button – the big red one at the right of the screen – to find out what you get for your cash.*

2

The package we're interested in is the first one, called Starter. This gives you 100MB of web space, which is more than adequate for a reasonable-sized website, and you also get full FTP access, webmail and some useful site statistics that help you see who's visiting your site, how they got there and where they came from.

3

Before you buy your hosting, though, you need a domain name. If you've shopped with 123reg before, login; if you haven't, you'll need to register. Once you've done that, click on Register and enter the domain name you'd like to use. Clicking on the Check Name button will show you whether that name is available in various flavours including .co.uk, .com and so on.

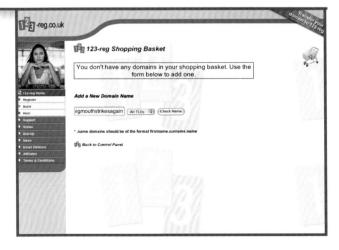

4

Although there are lots of different suffixes, there's no point in registering them all: a .co.uk address is perfect for the majority of British sites. Click on the domain you'd like to register and add it to your shopping basket.

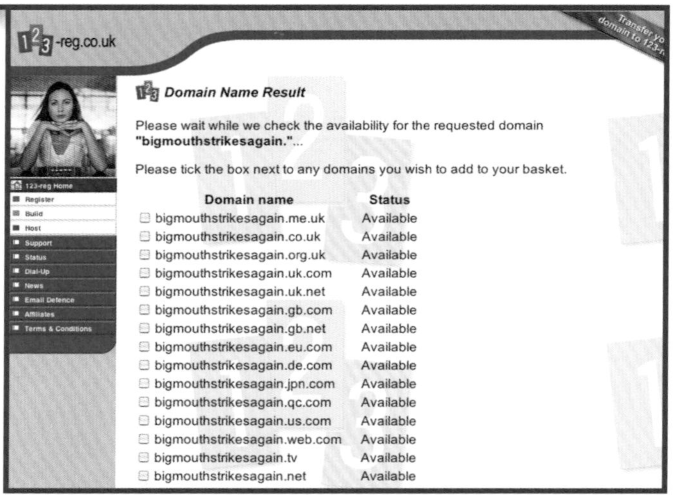

5

If you wish, you can register other domains at the same time. For now, though, we'll stick with one. If you've chosen a domain by mistake, you can get rid of it by clicking on the trashcan icon next to its name. Once you've got the domain you want in your shopping basket, click on Checkout to go to the next step.

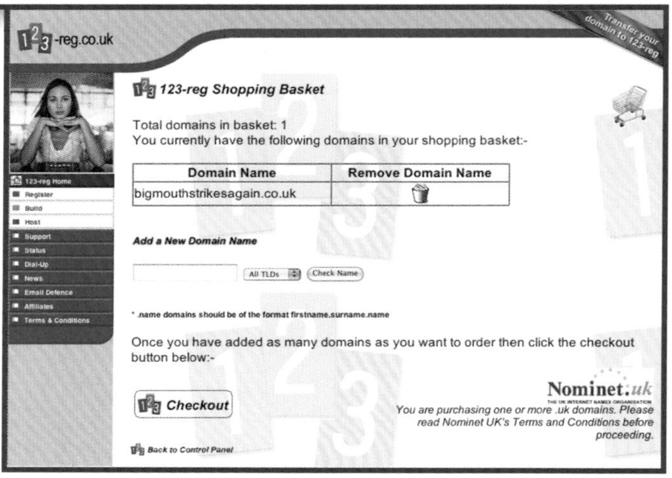

6

They're helpful people at 123reg, so when you order your domain name the site asks whether you want to add hosting. The answer is a big fat "no" – the two options you're given are among the firm's more expensive offerings, and we want something much cheaper. Make sure No Web Hosting is selected and then click the Next Step button.

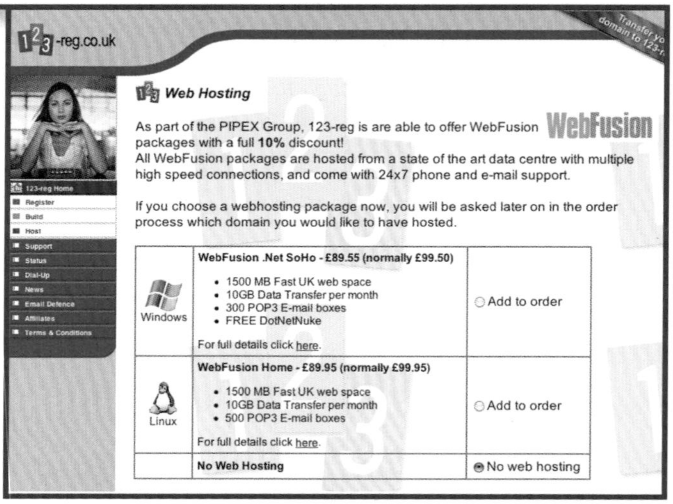

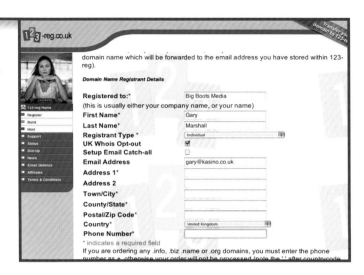

When you buy a domain name you need to provide personal details so that you can get your written certificate of ownership. This information is publicly available, so if you value your privacy you should check the UK Whois Opt-out button. This only applies to .uk domain names: you can't hide your details if you buy other kinds of domains.

123reg will now ask you for your credit or debit card details in order to complete the purchase. You'll notice that you're buying a domain name for 2 years rather than forever. This is because of the way the domain name system works. If you don't renew your domain name every two years, your registration will lapse and someone else can snap it up.

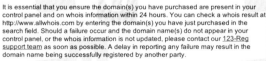

After a few seconds you should see a confirmation screen like the one in our screenshot. Although the site warns you that it could take up to 48 hours for your domain name to become fully active, in practice it's usually up and running in a few minutes. Don't worry if it takes a few hours or even a day, but contact your domain name provider if it's still not working at the end of the 48-hour period.

10

Now that you've got your domain name, it's time to attach some web space to it. You don't have to do it right now, but it only takes a few seconds so you might as well. To add web hosting to your new domain name, return to the 123reg control panel and look for the "Host" section. Click on "Host Your Own Website Now!" to begin the ordering process.

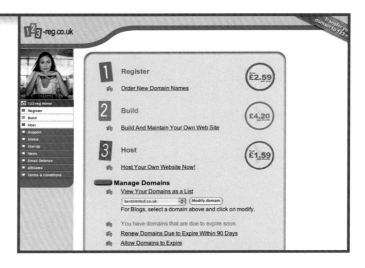

11

As you can see, there are lots of packages to choose from. We're going to go for the cheapest, which is called 123-reg Starter. Scroll down the page until you see the drop-down boxes, and in the first one choose the domain name to which you want to add hosting. Now, choose the hosting package (123-reg Starter) and choose a user name. Tick the "would you like to have your domain name..." box to automatically connect the domain name to your web space.

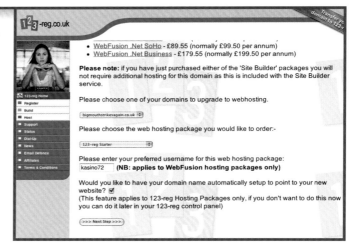

12

Once again, it's time to pay. You might notice that the £34.16 we've paid is rather more than the £1.59 per month advertised on the 123reg front page. That's because 123reg, like most firms, advertises its prices excluding VAT and excluding any setup fees. The cost of our year's hosting is £19.01, plus a £9.99 setup fee, plus VAT. It's rather sneaky but unfortunately almost every host seems to do it.

We have lift-off!

You've sorted out your hosting firm and you've bought a suitably snappy domain name. The final step is to create your web pages and stick them on your hosting firm's server. Once they're there, they'll be available to the entire internet.

As we'll discover in the following chapters, creating web pages is just as easy as writing a letter in a word processor or creating a new message in an email program. But how do you get the pages onto the internet when you've finished making them? The answer is FTP.

FTP is short for File Transfer Protocol and it's a way for computers to communicate with web servers. To use it you'll need a program called an FTP client, or you can use the online File Manager tools provided by many hosting firms. It sounds complicated but it's really straightforward: it's just a matter of logging in with the correct user name and password (the FTP system will be password protected to make sure that only you can update your site) and then dragging the files from your computer to the web server. And that's it!

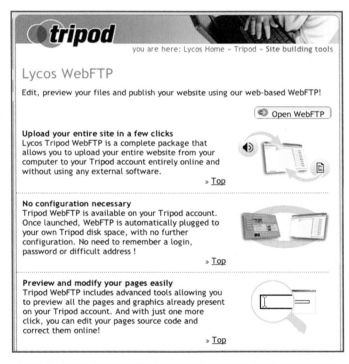

Most hosting firms provide FTP software that runs in your web browser and makes it easy to upload pages to the internet.

Top tip

Remember that when you buy a domain name, it's for a fixed period (usually two years) and you'll need to renew it when the expiry date approaches. The firm from which you bought your domain name will usually give you lots of notice, but if they don't or you forget to do anything then you might find that your chosen name has been snapped up by someone else – a competitor, perhaps, or someone doing something you don't approve of. That could be embarrassing if your Gran decides to visit your website and discovers it's been replaced with something filthy.

Designing a traditional site

In the very early days of the internet, you needed to know a special language to create web pages. This language was called HTML (HyperText Markup Language) and looked something like this:

```
<b>This text would appear in bold</b>
<i>This text would appear in italics</i>
```

It's actually very similar to the way word-processing software used to work, although of course these days you'd just click the Bold button to make your text bold. The good news is that the same thing has happened in website design, and there are plenty of programs that look and work pretty much like a word-processing program or a drawing program but which create the HTML pages that make up your site. Such programs are called WYSIWYG (pronounced "wizzywig"), which is short for What You See Is What You Get.

Web design programs

There are hundreds of web design programs on the market, but four packages dominate the market: Microsoft FrontPage, Macromedia Dreamweaver, Adobe GoLive and NVu. They're all designed to create anything from a simple web page to a giant online shop, but they do things in slightly different ways.

FrontPage
About £105 **www.microsoft.com**

As you'd expect from a Microsoft product, FrontPage looks and works like any other Windows program. In fact, it's very similar to Microsoft Word and doesn't take long to get to grips with. Although it's fine for beginners, it can also handle very complicated web design jobs and, if you pay for professional website hosting, it includes tools that you can use to manage your site and run systems such as online shops. However, it's pretty pricey and we think there are cheaper alternatives that do the job just as well.

Dreamweaver
About £290 **www.macromedia.com**

Dreamweaver is the firm favourite of professional website designers and it's an incredibly powerful program. However, that power means it can be pretty scary for web design beginners and it isn't cheap either. Unless you're planning to build a giant, complicated website and want to use all kinds of advanced features, it's probably too powerful for anyone putting together a personal site.

GoLive
About £390 **www.adobe.com**

GoLive is Adobe's rival to FrontPage and Dreamweaver but, while it's slightly easier to use than Macromedia's program, it has

Microsoft's FrontPage is designed to look and work like Microsoft Office, but it's best suited to professional web builders.

Dreamweaver is the world's most popular web design tool, but it's probably too complex – and too expensive – for building your first website.

Adobe's GoLive is a powerful design tool, but it's quite pricey and isn't as popular as Dreamweaver or FrontPage.

never attracted the same big audience. Its days may be numbered, too: Adobe recently bought Macromedia, which means it now owns both Dreamweaver and GoLive. One of them is likely to get the chop, and our money's on GoLive to go. Once again it's very powerful, but it's expensive and it's not a great idea to spend money on a program whose future is far from certain.

Nvu
Free **www.nvu.com**

Nvu looks and works in much the same way as FrontPage or GoLive, but there's one crucial difference: it's free. The people behind the program want as many people as possible to use it, so they decided to give it away rather than charge money. The only real downside to that approach is that there's no telephone number to call for technical support if you get stuck. However, the program itself is very straightforward and its help system can help you cope with the most common issues. We'll be using Nvu in our tutorials because it's available for both Windows and Apple Mac computers, it won't cost you a penny, and it's a great program.

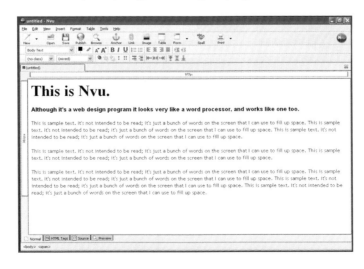

The free Nvu web design program is surprisingly powerful and you can't argue with a price tag of zero.

Other options

Depending on the hosting firm you've chosen, you might not need to use any additional software at all. More and more hosting firms now offer free tools to help their customers get started with web design. For example, if you sign up with Tripod you'll get access to its WebBuilder system. Other hosting firms – including paid-for hosting providers – offer similar tools.

So what do you get? Typically, hosting firms' tools are template-based. That means you'll be given a few pre-designed pages to choose from, and you can then edit the content of those pages to use your own text or your own photos. The benefit of this approach is that it's very quick and simple to use, but you shouldn't expect to create an all-singing, all dancing site. You'll find that the range of templates is fairly limited and there's only so much customisation you can do. Worse, it's likely to be very, very obvious that you've used a hosting firm's template to put your site together and your site will look very similar to many others.

There's another problem with online site design tools. You'll usually be offered a range of add-on such as guestbooks, visitor counters and other site accessories, but such goodies are considered to be rather naff by more experienced internet users.

That's because beginners often get carried away and end up putting every possible add-on into every single bit of their site, and the resulting pages aren't pretty. Have you ever seen teenagers in cars that appear to have the whole of Halfords glued to the boot? Such sites are the online equivalent.

Do it yourself

If you're in a hurry to get your words on the internet then there's no doubt that a free template-based system is the fastest way to do it. However, if you want to make a site that really sings then it's much better to use a program such as Nvu. There are a few reasons for this. First of all, the software's easy to use so it won't take long to get the hang of things. Secondly, you have complete control over every aspect of your site so if you don't like something, you can change it. But the most important reason is that as you get more confident, you'll become more ambitious. Once you've got the hang of putting together basic web pages you'll soon want to experiment with all kinds of bright ideas and snazzy sites, so it makes sense to use a program that can keep up with you when you start to spread your wings.

In the workshop that follows, we'll show you everything you need to get your very first pages on the World Wide Web.

Sites such as **www.Bravenet.com** offer lots of free add-ons for your site, but use them judiciously or you'll ruin your design.

PART ① **Building a basic web page**

In this workshop we'll put together a straightforward web page and make it available on the internet. To do this, we'll use the free Nvu program and some free web space from Tripod.co.uk. As you'll discover, putting your words on the web couldn't be easier.

①

It's a very good idea to create a new folder before you start building a web page, and to use this folder to save your work as you go along. In this example we've created a folder called "My website" on the Desktop. We've also identified a photograph we'd like to use in our page, so we've put the photo in our new folder so it's easy to find later on.

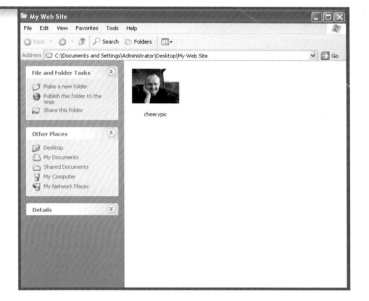

②

*Download the free Nvu web design program from **www.nvu.com** by going to the downloads page and clicking on the link for the appropriate installer (the Windows installer ends in .exe). When Windows asks you where you'd like to save the file, choose your Desktop. Once the file has downloaded, double-click on the Nvu installer icon on your Windows desktop to install the program.*

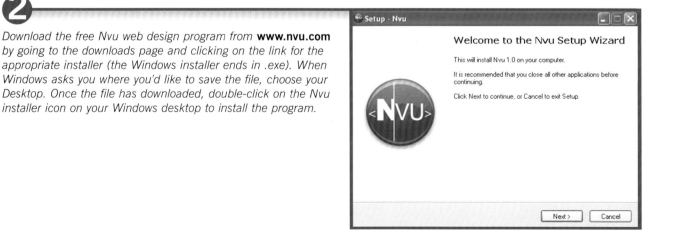

3

When the program has finished installing, click on Finish. Windows will now load Nvu for the very first time, and it should look like our screenshot. The window at the front is the Tips window and it's safe to close it. If you don't want to see the tips window ever again, un-tick the "Show Tips at Startup" box before closing the window.

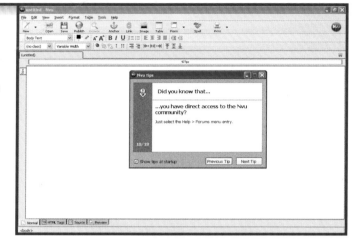

4

The main white window is where you create your web page. It works much like a word-processing program. You can change fonts and sizes, make text bold or italic, align text to the left, right or centre of the page, and so on. Try typing in some text and playing around with the Format menu and the Formatting toolbar to see the different things you can do.

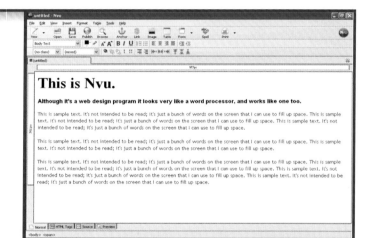

5

Once you've got the hang of things, delete the text you've been playing with. It's time to get serious! The first thing we need to do is to choose a colour scheme for our site. To do this, click on Format > Page Colors and Background (as Nvu is an American program, all the menus use American spellings).

6

Click on Use Custom Colours and you'll see boxes appear next to the labels "Normal Text", "Link Text" and so on. We'll leave the text colours as they are but choose a smart background colour for the page. To do this, click on the white rectangle next to the label "Background".

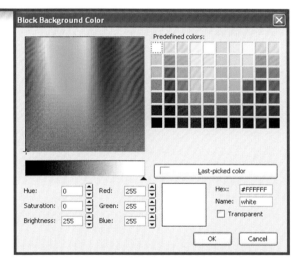

7

A new window will appear. This is the colour picker, and you can use it in three ways. You can choose a predefined colour by clicking one of the coloured blocks at the top right of the window, or you can use the rainbow-style box to find a more subtle colour. If you prefer, you can use the Hue, Saturation and Brightness or Red, Green and Blue controls to specify an exact colour.

8

In the predefined colours bit of the window, click on one of the dark red boxes and then on the OK button. This returns you to the Page Colors and Background window. We're finished with this for now, so click on OK to close the window and return to your page. If everything's gone according to plan, the entire page should be a dark red colour.

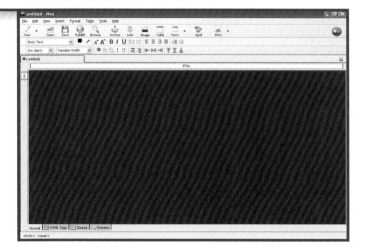

9

Although the red colour is rather nice, it's a bit dark if you intend to put text over it. One answer is to use a table that you can fill with text and, crucially, with another background colour. To add a table click the table button in the toolbar at the top of the Nvu window.

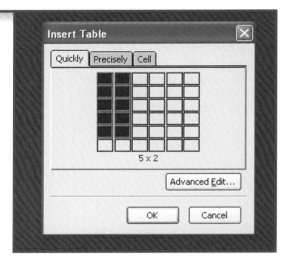

10

We'll use the simplest table possible: a table with one column and one row. To do this, click on the "Precisely" tab at the top of the dialog box and specify a table with one row, one column, a width of 80% of the window and a border of 2. Click OK when you've done this.

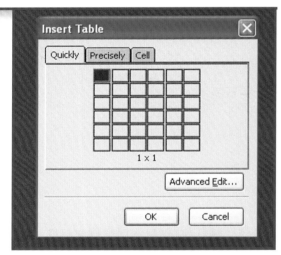

11

Nvu will return you to your page, and this time you'll see a wide, short rectangle. While it doesn't look very impressive just now we'll make a few changes to make it stand out. Click anywhere inside the box and then choose Table Properties from the Table menu.

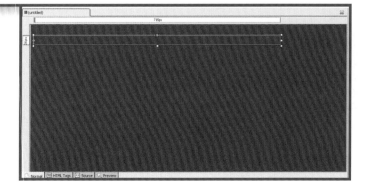

12

The first change we want to make is to have the table centred in the middle of the web page. To do this, look towards the bottom of the dialog box and select Center from the Table Alignment field. Now, click on the Background Color box and choose white from the colour picker. Close the colour picker and then click OK in the Table Properties dialog box.

13

Your screen should now look like this: the table should be white and should sit in the middle of the window instead of at the left of the screen. You can now start adding some text to your page. Click anywhere in the table, type your headlines and then press Enter a few times to add blank lines before typing the rest of your text.

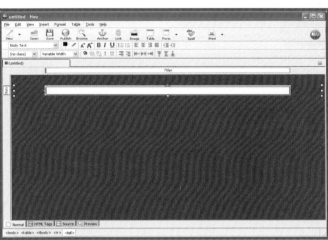

14

When you've added your text, use the Format menu to change the fonts and sizes in order to make your text more appealing. Avoid using weird-looking fonts, though, as they might not work properly on other people's computers. For best results we'd recommend Times, Arial or Verdana as these work on almost every machine.

15

Click on Save and Nvu will ask you to give your page a title. This isn't the file name, but rather the bit that will appear in the Title Bar of your visitors' browsers. Choose something reasonably descriptive and click OK. You'll now be asked to give your file a name. Call it "index" and save it in your website folder.

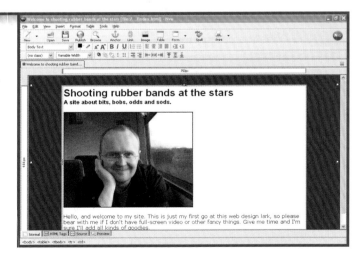

16

Let's add a picture. Click on Image and then use the Choose File button to find the photo you want to use. This picture should be located in the same folder on your computer as the web page you just saved (so copy it there now if necessary). Nvu will display a small preview of your image in the Image Properties dialog box. Before we move on, type a description of the image in the Alternative Text field. This will help partially-sighted people who visit your site and can't see images.

17

Let's give our picture a black border to make it stand out. Click on the Appearance tab and then type the number 2 in the "Solid Border" box. Click on OK and you should now see your image in your page. If it's in the wrong place you can move it by dragging and dropping, just as you'd move an image in a word-processing or desktop-publishing program.

18

The final step is adding a link. If you'd created several pages you'd link to them here, but for now we'll link to someone else's site – the BBC's. To do this, add some text at the bottom of your page, and be descriptive. "Click here" doesn't really say much, so we've typed "I haven't built the rest of my site yet, so here's the BBC site instead." Highlight the bit starting "here's" and click on the Link button in the toolbar.

Hello, and welcome to my site. This is just my first go at this web design lark, so please bear with me if I don't have full-screen video or other fancy things. Give me time and I'm sure I'll add all kinds of goodies.

I haven't built the rest of my site yet, so here's the BBC site instead.

19

In the Link Location field, type the full address of the page you'd like to link to. In this case, it's **http://www.bbc.co.uk**. If you were linking to a page on your own site you could miss out the web address altogether. Instead, you'd enter the page file name, such as page.htm, and then click on the URL Is Relative To Page Location box. URL is short for Uniform Resource Locator, which is a fancy way of saying "address". See p.128-9 for more on relative URLs.

Link Properties

Link Text
here's the BBC site instead.

Link Location
Enter a web page location, a local file, an email address, or select a Named Anchor or Heading from the popup list:

http://www.bbc.co.uk

☐ The above is an email address

☐ URL is relative to page location   Choose File...

▼ More Properties

Advanced Edit...

OK   Cancel   Help

20

Nvu will now take you back to your page, and you'll see that the text you highlighted has become an underlined link. Congratulations – you've made your first hyperlink! Now you've built your page, the next step is to publish it. We'll return to Nvu in a moment but for now, open your web browser and head for **www.tripod.co.uk**. It's time to get some web space.

s is just my first go at this web des

een video or other fancy things. Giv

et, so here's the BBC site instead.

PART **1**

Getting online with free web space

Signing up for free web space is simple, if a little time-consuming. Go to **www.tripod.co.uk** and then click on Join Tripod. This will take you to a page with a prominent "create your free account now!" link. If you click on this link you'll have to wade through the site terms and conditions, and you'll have to provide some basic details such as your name and address. You'll also need to choose a user name and password. Watch out for the small print: if you don't specify otherwise by ticking the appropriate boxes, Tripod will pass your details on to other firms so they can annoy you with ads (or as Tripod puts it, send you "exciting and useful information from Lycos Partners").

Once you've finished the sign-up procedure, Tripod will send you an email containing a website link. You need to click on this link to complete the registration process.

1

When you receive your email from Tripod, clicking on the included link will take you to the registration confirmation page. This will ask you to choose an FTP password. It's important that you take a note of whatever password you choose, as you'll use it whenever you upload pages to your Tripod web space.

tripod

you are here: Lycos Home – Tripod – Lycos Registration

Confirmation of your Lycos Tripod Registration

To have your Tripod account fully operational, you need to choose a sitename and an FTP Password. Your sitename is a part of the URL (wed address) for your site, in a http://members.lycos.co.uk/sitename/ format. FTP password is the password that will be required when publishing your site via an FTP software or FrontPage. FTP password can be the same as you Lycos Network password.

Sitename *	gsm191172
FTP password *	
confirm FTP password *	

To complete your registration, `75$0`
Please enter the security code *

(*) Mandatory field

[Next]

Return to Nvu and click Edit > Publishing Site Settings. Give your site a name, and then enter the following information:

Site address: **http://members.lycos.co.uk/username**
                           (where username is your Tripod user name)
Publishing address: **ftp://ftp.members.lycos.co.uk**
User name: your Tripod user name
Password: the password you chose in the previous step

Click on OK to return to your page. You're now ready to put it on the internet, so click on the Publish button. In the dialog box that appears, select the "include images and other files" box and then click Publish. Nvu will now display a progress dialog box to let you know what's going on. When you see "Publishing Completed", your page is on the internet.

Open your web browser and enter the address **http://members.lycos.co.uk/username***, where "username" is your Tripod user name. If everything's gone according to plan you should see a screen like this one, with your page and photo intact. Congratulations: you're online! Your carefully crafted page has been published on the World Wide Web for anyone to see.*

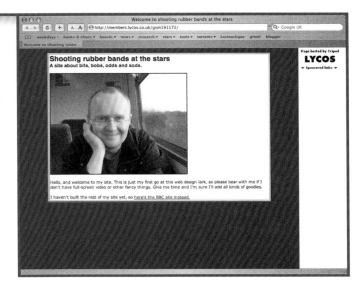

2

PART  # Building bigger sites

Smart planning

As we've discovered, it's easy to put together a few pages and put them on the web. However, when you're building bigger sites, it's a very good idea to do some planning before you reach for your web design program. A little bit of forward thinking can save you a great deal of time and effort, and it can prevent you having to rebuild an entire site from scratch later on.

The most important weapon in any web designer's arsenal isn't a fast computer or a powerful program: it's a bit of paper and a pencil. Use them to create an outline of your site that details the pages your site will include, and what you'll call them. If you're the artistic type you can also sketch out a rough design for your site, which will save you a bit of time when it comes to putting the actual pages together.

Thinking ahead

To create your site outline, you need to know what your site is going to do – which means knowing who your audience will be. For example, if you're building a site to show off your photography skills, then your visitors will want to see your pictures. A sensible site structure might look a bit like this:

- Home page
- About me page
- Portrait photography
- Landscape photography
- Arty photography

That's a fairly simple example, but you could expand on it like this:

- Home page
- About me page
- Portrait photography
   Children
   Families
   Celebrities
- Landscape photography
   UK
   Europe
   USA
- Arty photography

What's good about this way of doing things is that you can see at a glance what pages you need and what links you'll need to have on your pages. So for example, our photographer might need the following pages:

File name	Purpose of page
Index.html	Home page
About.html	About Me page
Portrait.html	Portrait photography: main page
Kidportraits.html	Portraits: children
Familyportraits.html	Portraits: family
Celebportraits.html	Portraits: celebrities
Landscape.html	Landscape photography: main page
UKland.html	Landscapes: UK
Euroland.html	Landscapes: Europe
USAland.html	Landscapes: USA

As you can see, by scribbling a rough site structure on a bit of paper our photographer can see that he or she needs to create ten distinct web pages.

A rough sketch on paper is the essential first step en route to the web.

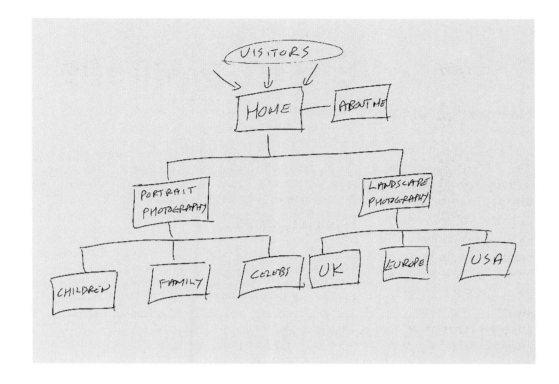

Oh, goodies

There are stacks of sites that offer all kinds of add-ons for your site, and you'll find that many web design programs also include things called "widgets", "smart objects" or something similar. Typically these are little bits of code that you can add to your site. Examples include:

- Discussion forums
- Guest books
- Calendars
- Little buttons saying "made with…"
- Visitor statistics
- Special effects

It's tempting to add such items to your site, but it's important to choose any goodies carefully. In many cases add-ons can make your site look worse rather than better, so for example if you have a discussion board that nobody uses, visitors will get a much worse impression of your site than if you didn't have a discussion forum at all.

The same applies to many other add-ons. Calendars are often useless, little buttons saying "I made this site with…" are rather naff, and special effects are almost always a bad idea. For example, you can get a special effect that takes a picture and adds what looks like a moving, watery reflection immediately below it, but the code to make this happen takes forever to download and the effect itself has long since fallen out of fashion.

The golden rule of goodies is "if in doubt, leave it out".

eFreeGuestbooks Demo Book

Please do not post support questions in this book, we do not respond to support questions posted here

Sign eFreeGuestbooks Demo Book   Return to eFreeGuestbooks

Entry #: 991	
Name:	ssssssssssss
Email:	Protected
Site Rating:	10
Comments: ◉	
XXXXXXXXXXXXXXXXXXXXXXXXXXXXXXXXXXXXXXXXXXXXXXXXXXXXXXXXXXXXXXXXXXXXXXXXXXXXXXXXXXXXXXXXXXXXXXXXXXXX	

Entry #: 990	
Name:	dude
Site Rating:	10
Comments:	testing . . .

Entry #: 989	
Private Entry ⚿	

Entry #: 988	
Name:	John
Web Site:	Silvertrain

Free add-ons such as guestbooks may be tempting, but as you can see they often look appalling.

Everyone's a winner

There's no big secret to building a successful site. All you need to know are two very straightforward rules: the KISS rule and the two-click rule.

KISS stands for "keep it simple and straightforward" and it's what differentiates good sites from bad ones. Sites that make visitors endure a pointless animation before taking them to the home page have forgotten the KISS rule, and their visitors are likely to head off for another site long before the animation has finished loading.

With the internet, less is more: a few well-chosen images will have more impact on a page than hundreds of flashing buttons, and a few paragraphs of simple, well-written text will be easier to read and more attractive to the eye than endless blocks of tiny type.

The two-click rule is particularly important if you're trying to sell things, but it applies to any kind of site. It's a simple rule that makes a big difference, and it says:

"Visitors should be able to find what they're looking for with just two mouse clicks."

In the case of our photographer's site, that means people should be able to find the photos they want to see with two mouse clicks. Does our rough site structure follow that rule? It does: to get to portraits of children, for example, visitors need only click the "children" link and then the photo they want to see.

The two-click rule works just as well on giant sites as it does on small ones. If you're buying a new TV online, you'll find that even the biggest electrical sites enable you to find TVs by clicking Audio-Visual and then Televisions.

With really big sites, the two-click rule usually means that visitors should be able to find the appropriate product category in two clicks, rather than a specific product. In our TV example above, two clicks does indeed take you to the TV section of an electrical site, but instead of seeing the entire range of televisions – which could run to hundreds of different products – you'll then see links for different kinds of TVs: portable TVs, standard TVs, widescreen TVs, LCD TVs, Plasma TVs, projector TVs and so on. Using categories like this is the best way to combine the two-click rule with the KISS rule.

If you're planning to include lots and lots of content in your site, spend a bit of time browsing similar sites to get an idea of how they organise their pages. Such browsing will give you a really good idea of how to organise your own site, which will save you a lot of time and an awful lot of effort.

Sites such as **www.Comet.co.uk** follow the two-click rule. So, for example, if you want to buy a TV, you'd click "Televisions" and then the particular type of TV you're looking for.

FreeFoto.com is a great source of images that you can use in your site, and if it's a non-profit site you can use the images free of charge.

Copyrights and wrongs

A picture's worth a thousand words, but what if you don't have any pictures? If you're not a photographer, how do you get some images for your site?

Unfortunately, getting pictures for your website isn't as simple as doing a Google Image Search (**http://images.google.com**), finding what you want and then adding it to your site. Most images you'll see online are protected by copyright, which means that only the owner of those images has the right to make copies of them. Infringing copyright is illegal, and if you're caught doing it you'll be forced to remove the offending images at best, or sued silly at worst.

Don't despair, though, because there are lots of places where you can get free, high-quality images legally. One of our favourites is FreeFoto (**www.freefoto.com**), which at the time of writing boasts 74,630 images in 2,577 categories. There are pictures of UK landmarks, of spectacular weather, of animals… if you can imagine it, FreeFoto probably has a photo of it.

High quality photographs for free – surely there's a catch? There is, but it's not a scary one. You're allowed to use FreeFoto's images only for private, non-commercial use, so if you're making money from your site then you'll have to pay for your pictures. However, for home or charity sites, you can use as many FreeFoto images as you like provided that you credit the site on your home page and provide a link back to the FreeFoto site.

Another good source of content is the Creative Commons site at **http://creativecommons.org**. Here you'll find all kinds of things – photos, music and even movies – put together by people who want to share their work with others. Each image (or music file, or movie) will come with a Creative Commons licence that tells you exactly what you can and cannot do with it, so for example you'll find lots of images that you can use on your own site provided you don't modify the images or try to pass them off as your own work.

Writing for the web

It's amazing how many people create beautiful-looking websites and then ruin them with giant blocks of tiny, hard-to-read text. For most sites the text is the important bit, so it's important to get it right.

Reading text on a computer screen is very different from reading printed text. While a newspaper will happily put 1,000 words of densely packed type on a single page – and newspaper buyers will happily read it – the same text on a web page would look horrible and intimidating. Internet readers tend to have shorter attention spans than newspaper readers, too, so too much text is a no–no.

There are two things to consider when you're writing text for the web: what you're saying, and how it looks. Here are our top tips:

Keep it short

Simple, punchy sentences will be much more effective than really long sentences, which use lots of interruptions (some with commas, some with brackets and some – or even many – with dashes) and tend to drag on a lot; in many cases you could chop 75% of the sentence out and still make sense.

Jargon is junk

This is a particular peril in the world of business websites, where far too many firms call a spade a metallic gardening implement and sandwich firms "provide portable meal solutions". Call a spade a spade!

Break it up

This:

Too busy to shop? We can help. Tell us what you want and we'll:

- Find the perfect product
- Get it at the best possible price
- Deliver it to your door

100% Safe Shopping guarantee – click here to find out more!

Is better than this:

Too busy to shop? We can help. Tell us what you want and we'll find the perfect product, get it at the best possible price and deliver it to your door. Our Safe Shopping Guarantee means you can shop with confidence; click here to find out more.

Web users are a bit like magpies: they look at the shiny things first. On a web page that means your visitors' eyes will be attracted to headlines, to bullet points and to anything highlighted rather than to solid blocks of text.

Short paragraphs with text broken by clear lines and if necessary spread over two or more pages makes reading on the web a more pleasurable experience.

A few simple things can make a big difference. For example, a single blank line between paragraphs makes text feel a lot less cluttered, and a half-dozen short paragraphs looks much friendlier than two very long ones. If you're publishing really long bits of text, such as essays, articles or long rants about the evils of traffic wardens, then consider splitting the text over a few pages. You'll find that many newspaper sites do this.

Choose your colours

Most of the things we read tend to use dark text on a light background, and with good reason: it's easy on the eyes. Only use unusual colour combinations if you're absolutely sure what you're doing, or you could end up with text that looks pretty from a distance but which makes your visitors' eyes bleed when they actually try to read it.

Fix your fonts

The KISS rule applies to your fonts as well as the overall design of your site. We'd recommend sticking to a maximum of two different fonts: one for headlines, and one for the main text.

Some fonts work better online than others. For example, clean fonts such as Arial, Verdana and Georgia were designed for on-screen viewing and unsurprisingly work very well. Other fonts – particularly gimmicky ones – are hard to read, and may not be present on your visitors' computers. If in doubt, go with the tried and tested typefaces.

Think about search engines

Most search engines analyse the content of pages, so it's a good idea to think of the search terms people might use to find sites like yours. For example, if you're a portrait photographer then you'd expect people to search for sites like yours by using terms such as "portrait photographer London", "family photographs" or something similar. Using these terms in your site's body text will improve your site's visibility in search engine results.

Newspaper sites use black text on white backgrounds because it's very easy to read. Avoid dark backgrounds and light coloured text.

43

Getting on Google

If the search engine Google doesn't know about your site, it might as well not exist. Google will normally find your site without any intervention from you, but there are a few tricks you can use to make your site more Google-friendly.

We've already mentioned that you should include suitable search terms in your pages' text, but you should also try the following:

Use an appropriate title

Google (and other search engines) will display your page title in their search results, so it's a good idea to give each page a descriptive title. For example, "My first site" won't be as effective as "pictures of my black Labrador". Use a different title for each page, so for example in the case of our photographer, one page might be titled "Joe Bloggs: Portrait photography" and another might be "Joe Bloggs: Landscape photography."

Enter a description

Most web design programs enable you to insert a description into your page, usually in the Page Properties section. This doesn't appear anywhere on your site, but it is visible to search engines and it's what appears immediately below your page title in search results. Use this section to describe who you are or what your site is.

For example, our photographer might write: "Joe Bloggs is a portrait and landscape photographer based in London, specialising in pictures of children and families".

Get linked

The more popular a site, the more important Google thinks it is and the higher it will appear in search engine results. One way in which Google judges popularity is by looking at the sites that link to a particular page, so if you can persuade people to link to you then your site will rise up the search engine rankings.

You can find out more about Google site listings at **www.google.co.uk/intl/en/webmasters/**, which is an excellent collection of how-to articles.

Google has an extensive help section that tells you everything you need to know about getting your site listed in its giant database – and what dirty tricks will get your site blacklisted.

Google Information for Webmasters

Home

About Google

Webmaster Info
FAQ
Guidelines
Facts & Fiction
SEOs
Googlebot
Removals

Find on this site:

[Search]

Welcome Webmasters

If you are responsible for a website, the following information may be of interest to you. We hope you find it helpful.

How do I get my site listed on Google?

1. The basics.
2. Submitting a site.

My webpages have never been included in the Google index.

1. My site's new to the web, and I recently submitted it.
2. My site's been live for a few months.
3. Some of my pages are included, but others are missing.

My webpages used to be listed and now they aren't.

1. I have not changed anything, I promise.
2. There may have been a problem on my end.

My site's listing is incorrect and I need it changed.

1. My information is outdated.
2. I migrated my website to a new URL.
3. There is no description of my site.
4. The description of my site is wrong in the results.

I am puzzled by my site's ranking.

1. How Google ranks pages.
2. My page's location in the search results keeps changing.
3. My pages do not return for certain keywords.

For other topics, please see the sections on the left side of this page. You may also be interested in our Advanced Questions area.

If you have still not found answers to your questions, you might try the User Support Discussion Forum, a Google Groups forum for sharing and gaining expertise in Google services.

Google AdSense for Web Publishers
Publish ads that match your content, help visitors find related products and services – and maximise your ad revenue. Learn more.

Become a Google Advertising Professional
Get free online training and tools designed to make you a better client manager. Learn more.

Showcase your products for free on Froogle
Bring online shoppers directly to your product pages through Froogle, Google's product search engine. Learn more.

©2005 Google - Home - About Google - We're Hiring - Site Map

PART 2

Bigger and better site building

We've already explored the basics of site building, and we've looked at the importance of planning. Here we'll bring the two together and see how to build a bigger site.

For this workshop we've decided to build an online portfolio, a kind of digital CV. With our trusty pen and paper we've worked out that we need the following pages:

- The home page – the front page of the site;
- A magazine page, to cover magazine work;
- A book page, to talk about books;
- A TV and radio page, to talk about broadcasting;
- A music page, to cover music.

In addition to these pages, we also need a way to contact the portfolio's owner. We'll do that by email, so that's a sixth link.

We've stopped at six pages for the sake of clarity, but the approach we'll take works just as well for sites with 60 pages as it does for six. In this workshop, we'll come up with the basic design for our site and then we'll save it as a template. By doing this we can quickly create additional pages that use our design and we can do it without having to painstakingly recreate the design each and every time. As we'll discover, templates are a big timesaver.

Once again, we've stuck with the open source Nvu program, which is easy to use and free of charge. You can of course use any web editing program to build a site, but we think Nvu is the perfect starting point for web design newcomers.

Before you begin to build a site, create a new folder for all your site files. If there are images you plan to use in your pages, collect them and put them in the folder before you begin to build any pages. This will save you a great deal of time and effort in the long run. In this screenshot we've created a big logo, which we'll use in our site.

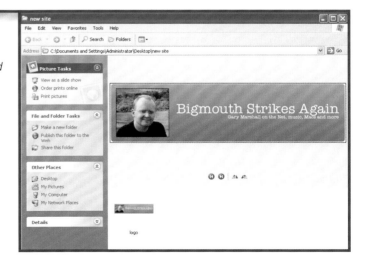

②

Launch Nvu and close the Tips dialog box if it appears. The first step is to save your page in your site folder, so do this and give your page a title when prompted. Choose something descriptive, as this will appear at the top of your visitors' web browsers. By keeping all your pages and images in the same folder, it will make creating links and adding images much, much easier.

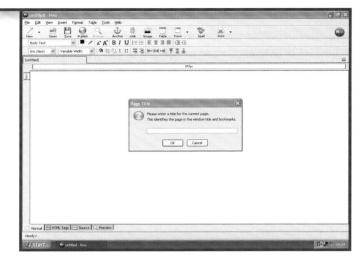

③

The first page you create in any site is likely to be the home page, and this site is no exception. By default web browsers look for the page "index.html" in any site, so your home page should use that name too. Type "index" (without the inverted commas) in the File name box and then click Save; Nvu will add the ".html" bit automatically.

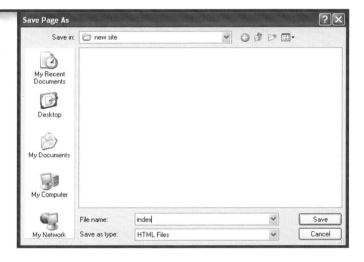

④

The easiest way to build an attractive layout is to use a table. Click on the Table icon in the toolbar and use your mouse to draw a 3 x 3 table (three rows and three columns). Click OK when you've done this and you should now see an empty table on your page.

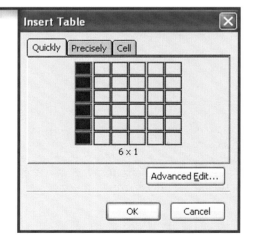

5

When you create a table in Nvu, it makes the table width 80% of the screen. If you'd like to make your table narrower or wider it's just a matter of selecting the table and then using the mouse to drag a corner left or right, depending on whether you want to make the table narrower or wider.

6

The layout we'll use for our page isn't quite as simple as a 3 x 3 table; we want a single row at the top, three columns below it and then a single row below that. To turn the top row into a single table cell, highlight all three cells in the row and then right click on them. Click on Join Selected Cells to turn three cells into one.

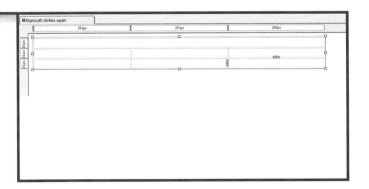

7

Your table should now look like the one in our screenshot, with a single column spanning the entire table and then two three-column rows below it. Let's repeat the process with the bottom row: highlight the three cells, right-click and then click Join Selected Cells.

8

Your table should look like this: one wide column, three narrow columns and then one wide column. This table will ensure that each bit of our site appears in the right place. Don't worry about the size of the rows just yet: as we put things into the table, the rows will automatically expand to fit the images or text that we place in them.

9

Click on Format > Page Colors and Background and you should see this dialog box. Click on the button next to Use Custom Colours and then click on the coloured box labelled Background. Nvu will now display the colour palette; choose the colour you want to use, click OK and then click OK to return to your page. In this example we've gone for a light grey background colour.

Page Colors and Background

Page Colors

○ Reader's default colors (Don't set colors in page)

◉ Use custom colors:

Normal text: ■   Normal text

Link text: ■   Link text

Active link text: ■   Active link text

Visited link text: ■   Visited link text

Background: ☐

Background Image:

☐ URL is relative to page location   Choose File...

Advanced Edit...

OK   Cancel

10

By default tables are transparent, so the colour of the page background will also be the colour of the table. A simple and effective trick is to make your table a different colour from the page background, so for example our page would look better with a white table on the grey background. This is easy to do: click on the table and then choose Table > Table Properties.

11

At the very bottom of the dialog box you'll see a box labelled Background Colour. Click on this to see the colour palette, and then choose the colour you'd like to use. If you click on the Apply button rather than the OK button you can see the results without closing the dialog box, which is handy if you want to try a number of different colours to see which one works best. Click OK when you're happy.

Table Properties

Table

Size

Rows: 3   Height: ☐   % of window ▾

Columns: 3   Width: 80   % of window ▾

Borders and Spacing

Border: 2   pixels

Spacing: 0   pixels between cells

Padding: 10   pixels between cell border and content

Table Alignment: Center ▾   Caption: None ▾

Background Color: ☐

Advanced Edit...

OK   Apply   Cancel   Help

12

In this example we've made the table background white, which works well on top of our page's light grey background. Don't worry, we'll add some colour too – in fact, we'll do it now by adding a big image to the page. Click in the top row of your table and then click on the Image button in the main toolbar.

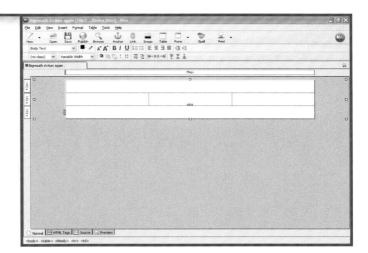

13

Locate the image you want to use by clicking Choose File and then navigating to the appropriate image (which should be in the site folder we created earlier). In the Alternative Text field, type a short description of what the image is: this means your site will be more accessible to people who can't or don't browse with images enabled. Don't click OK just yet.

14

Most of us expect the logo of a site to be clickable, and we expect it to take us to the front page if we do click on it. Making your image do this is simple enough: click on the Link tab and then type the name of the page you want your image to link to. In most cases that will be index.html. Make sure that the "Show border around linked image" box isn't ticked and then click OK.

15

Nvu will take you back to the main editing window, where your image should appear. Your site is starting to look like a proper site! If you've placed your image in the wrong bit of the table by mistake, don't worry: simply drag it using the mouse and drop it in its rightful place.

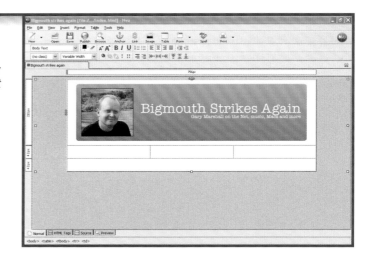

16

Type a short bit of descriptive text in each column so that you can see at a glance what each bit of your table will contain. When you do this, you may notice that – as in our case – the text isn't quite where you want it to be. In our screenshot the text of the middle column is a little too far to the right, and would look better if it moved slightly to the left.

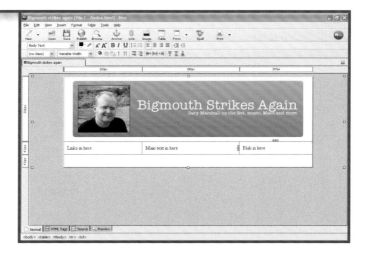

17

Our column is easy to adjust: click anywhere inside the column and at the top of the editing window, you'll see three bars with a number in each. These bars show the edges and sizes of each column. To resize the middle column, grab the line between the first and second bar and then drag it to the left. Let go when it's in the right place and your columns will automatically resize.

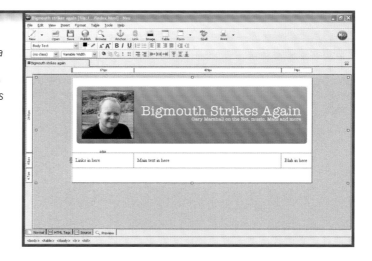

18

The left hand column will contain more than one link, so add the word "Link" a few more times with each occurrence on a new blank line. When you do this you'll notice something strange happen: as your columns get longer, the text in the other two columns starts to move. That's because Nvu is trying to position it in the centre of each column. This is something we'll need to change.

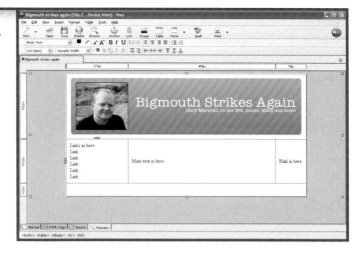

19

To change the position of text within your table, select the cells you want to change and then click Table > Table Properties. The section you need is the Content Alignment section, which is about halfway down the screen on the right-hand side. We want to change the Vertical Alignment, so click on the box next to Vertical and then select Top. Click OK and your page's text should now start at the top of each column rather than in the middle.

Link Properties

Link Text
here's the BBC site instead.

Link Location
Enter a web page location, a local file, an email address, or select a Named Anchor or Heading from the popup list:

http://www.bbc.co.uk

☐ The above is an email address
☐ URL is relative to page location   Choose File...

▼ More Properties

Advanced Edit...

OK   Cancel   Help

20

Many sites include a copyright notice at the bottom of each page, and our site will too. Click in the bottom cell of your table to position the cursor. Now, we'll need to insert a special character – the © symbol – because the copyright symbol isn't present on most keyboards. To bring up the Insert Character screen, click Insert > Characters and Symbols.

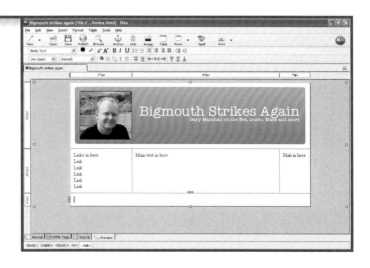

21

The copyright symbol lives in the Common Symbols collection, along with other common characters such as the trademark sign and so on. Make sure the Common Symbols option is selected in the "Category" box. In the right hand drop-down, scroll until you find the copyright symbol. Click Insert to add that symbol to your page.

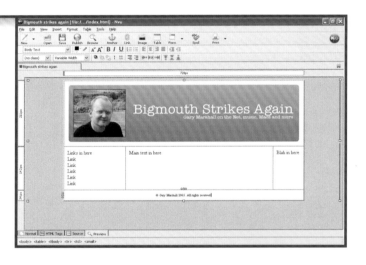

22

The copyright symbol should appear in the appropriate place, and you can now add the rest of your text. For footers like this it's a good idea to make the font size a little bit smaller than the rest of your text. To do this, highlight the text in the footer and click the Reduce Font icon (it's on the second-bottom toolbar and looks like a little capital A).

23

It should always be clear where a link will take someone, and "link" isn't exactly descriptive. Replace each occurrence of the word "link" with something more meaningful, but try to keep it short. For example, instead of "a page about music" the word "music" will do just fine. It's a good idea to make your very first link a "Home" link that takes visitors to the front page of your site.

Highlight the first would-be link in the column (in this example, "Home") and then click the Link button in the top toolbar. In the white box, enter the file name of the page you want to link to. It's very important that you get the name exactly right and that you include the ".html" bit at the end, or the link won't work. Click OK and repeat the process for your other links.

Link Properties

Link Text
Home

Link Location
Enter a web page location, a local file, an email address, or select a Named Anchor or Heading from the popup list:

index.html

☐ The above is an email address

☐ URL is relative to page location   Choose File...

▼ More Properties

Advanced Edit...

OK   Cancel   Help

You can add email links as well as page links. The only difference is that instead of a page file name, you type the appropriate email address instead. Make sure you tick the "The above is an email address" box before clicking OK. Now, when visitors click on that link it will automatically open their email program and create a new, blank email to that address.

Link Properties

Link Text
Contact

Link Location
Enter a web page location, a local file, an email address, or select a Named Anchor or Heading from the popup list:

gary@kasino.co.uk

☑ The above is an email address

☐ URL is relative to page location   Choose File...

▼ More Properties

Advanced Edit...

OK   Cancel   Help

That's the navigation section finished; now, the actual page content. In the middle column, type some sample text. It doesn't matter what you type, as we're only going to use this text to help us come up with a layout. We'll replace the text later. When you've finished adding your text, highlight the headline but not the rest of your text.

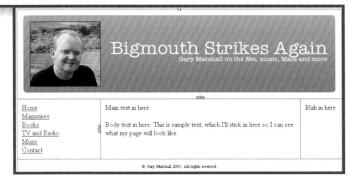

27

A headline isn't much use if it doesn't stand out, and there's a very easy way to make it do just that. Once you've highlighted your headline, click on the style drop-down at the very left of the lower toolbar – it will say "(no class)". From the available options, choose Heading 1.

28

As if by magic, the headline becomes bigger and bolder. Try experimenting with the different heading types: they're numbered in order from biggest to smallest, so heading 1 is the biggest size and heading 6 is the smallest. For most sites, heading 1 is best suited to major headlines, with heading 2 for sub-headings and so on.

29

By default Nvu adds text in Times New Roman, which looks a little old-fashioned. Changing the fonts on your page is easy: select your table and then click on the Font drop-down (it's the second box in the very bottom toolbar) or use the Format > Font menu. In this screenshot we've gone for Helvetica/Arial, which looks modern and clean and which works in every web browser.

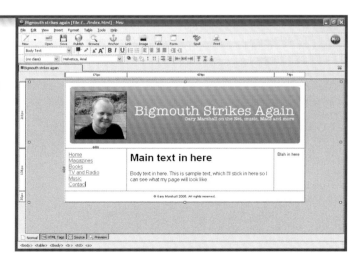

30

We started off with three columns of text, but the far right column isn't really necessary. No problem: we can delete an individual column by clicking on it. You should see three little images appear at the top of the column: a left arrow, a circled X, and a right arrow. Click on the X button and the redundant column will disappear. The main column will expand to fill the gap.

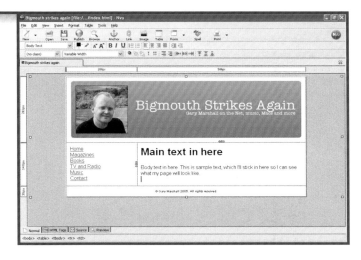

31

It's time to see how the page will look in a web browser. To do this, click on File > Browse Page to launch your web browser. When prompted, save your page; after a few seconds it will load in your web browser. This is exactly as your site will appear on the internet. As you can see there's a problem: the table cell borders have appeared, but we don't want to see them.

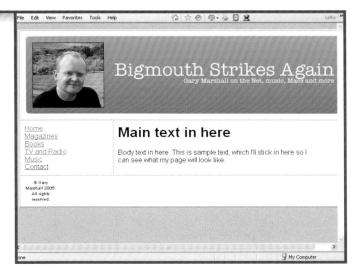

32

Why do borders appear in your web browser when they're only just visible in Nvu? The reason is because a size has been specified for the borders: by default, Nvu tables have borders that are two pixels wide. Many browsers including Internet Explorer will take this size and draw the borders on screen, whether you want them or not. To change this, select the entire table and then click Table > Table Properties.

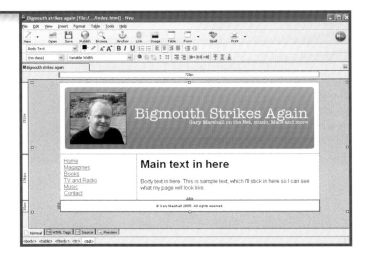

To get rid of the borders, we need to change their width to zero. To do this, look for the Borders and Spacing section and change Border to zero. If spacing isn't already set to zero, change it too. If you wish, you can increase the Padding value to add more space between your (now-invisible) borders and the contents of your table, although we'll leave the setting as it is for now.

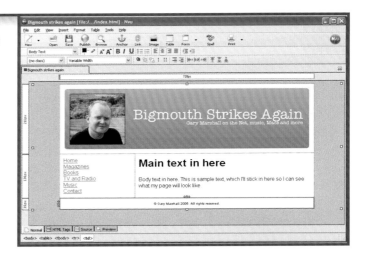

Click OK to close the dialog box. Don't worry if your page doesn't seem to have changed: because the border colour hasn't been set, your borders are shown in red lines so that you can see where they are even when you've set the border size to zero. In order to see your page as it will look in a web browser, click File > Browse Page. Click OK if Nvu asks you to save the page.

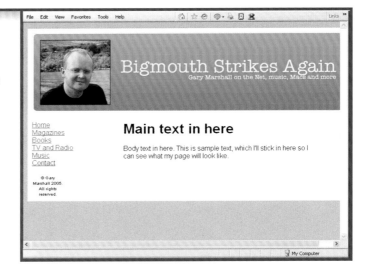

Your page should now load in your web browser, and if everything's gone according to plan then you shouldn't be able to see the borders of your table cells. (Eagle-eyed readers will see that our footnote has moved to the left of the screen. This is because of a bug in our web browser; the footnote should appear in the correct place when you view it in your own web browser.)

36

Now that the page looks exactly the way we want it to look, save the file again. We're going to save it twice: first as a normal web page, and then as a template. Saving a page as a template is a big time-saver, as we'll discover in the next few steps. To do it, click Format and then Page Title and Properties. Click the "This Page is a template" box and then click OK.

Page Properties

General information
Location: file:///C:/Documents%20and%20Setti...tor/Desktop/new%20site/index.html
Last Modified: 05 September 2005 16:55:08
Title: Bigmouth strikes again
Author:
Description:

Templates
☑ This page is a template

Internationalization
Language: Choose a language
Writing direction: No direction specified
Character set: ISO-8859-1   Choose a charset

Advanced users:
To edit other contents of the <head> region, use "HTML Source" in the View Menu or Edit Mode Toolbar.

OK   Cancel

37

Nvu will return you to the main editing window. Click on File > Save As and navigate to the folder for your new website. You'll see that the Save As Type drop-down now says "HTML templates": give your template a suitably descriptive name and then click Save. Nvu will now save your page as a template that you can re-use again and again.

Save Page As

Save in: new site

My Recent Documents
Desktop
My Documents
My Computer
My Network

File name: bigmouth template   Save
Save as type: HTML templates   Cancel

38

Now we'll add some more pages to our site. At the very top left of the Nvu screen – on the main toolbar – you'll see an icon with the label "New", and you'll see that there's a small arrow on the right of this icon. Click on the arrow, choose More Options and then select "A new document based on a template". Choose the template you saved in the previous step.

Choose File

Look in: new site

bigmouth template
index
logo

My Recent Documents
Desktop
My Documents
My Computer
My Network

File name: bigmouth template   Open
Files of type: All Files   Cancel

Nvu will now create your new page, but unlike normal new pages it will contain all the bits and pieces you put in your template. As you can see, it's a great way to speed up site design when you're using the same items on every page, because you don't have to painstakingly recreate the tables, add links or import images.

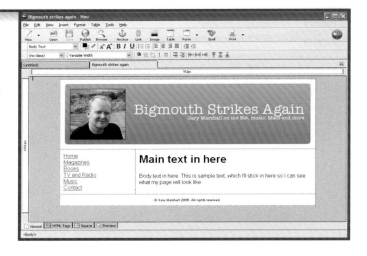

You'll find that if you try to replace any of your text, Nvu won't let you. This is because your page is still attached to the template, and as a result it won't let you edit anything that's in the original template. If you click on Edit and select Detach From Template you'll now be able to replace the original headline with a new headline, as we've done in our screenshot.

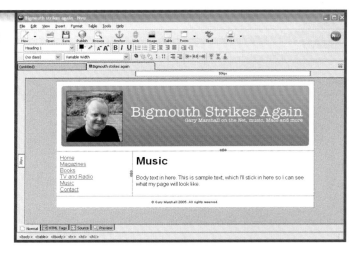

Now you can replace the body text with the text you actually want to use in your page. For best results, keep your paragraphs as short as you can and space them out with a blank line between each one. Don't make the text too small, either: if your visitors see what appears to be a giant block of small print, it's likely to intimidate them. Keep checking your site in your web browser to make sure it's clear, clean and legible.

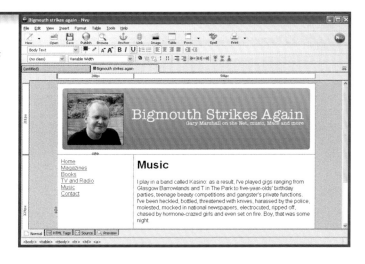

Good navigation bars let visitors see exactly where they are in the site. One of the simplest ways to do this is to replace the link for the current page (in this case, "Music") with plain text and to prefix the text with a jaggy bracket and a space. To do this just highlight the link, press Delete and then type the replacement text – "> Music".

Home
Magazines
Books
TV and Radio
> |Music
Contact

When you've finished putting your page together, click on Save As to save it to your hard disk. Remember to use exactly the same file name that you used in your site's links section and to save the file in the same folder as your other pages, or your finished site won't work. In this example our page about music is called "music.html". Nvu adds the ".html" bit automatically.

Save Page As

Save in: new site

index

My Recent Documents

Desktop

My Documents

My Computer

File name: music

Save as type: HTML Files

Save

Cancel

My Network

It's always a good idea to make your pages as search engine-friendly as possible. Click Format > Page Title and Properties and give each page a unique title and description. This makes your site much clearer to sites such as Google, and it ensures that when your site appears in search engine results, you'll see a different title and description for each of your pages. Save your page again and then follow the same procedure for each remaining page in your site.

Page Properties

General information
Location: file:///C:/Documents%20and%20Setti...tor/Desktop/new%20site/music.html
Last Modified: 05 September 2005 17:02:52

Title: Bigmouth strikes again: Music
Author:
Description: Freelance journalism about technology, music and more

Templates
☐ This page is a template

Internationalization

Language: _____ [Choose a language]

Writing direction: No direction specified ▾

Character set: ISO-8859-1 [Choose a charset]

Advanced users:
To edit other contents of the <head> region, use "HTML Source" in the View Menu or Edit Mode Toolbar.

OK   Cancel

45

Your ISP or hosting firm will provide you with FTP details for publishing pages to your Web space. In Nvu, click Edit > Publishing Site Settings and enter the appropriate details. Be particularly careful with user names and passwords: if you mistype them, you won't be able to access your Web space.

Publish Settings ✕

Publishing Sites
My web site

[New Site]
[Set as Default]
[Remove Site]

Site Name: My web site

Web Site Information
HTTP address of your homepage (e.g.: 'http://www.myisp.com/myusername'):
http://www.bigmouthstrikesagain.co.uk

Publishing Server
Publishing address (e.g.: 'ftp://ftp.myisp.com/myusername'):
ftp://hosting5.123-reg.co.uk   [Select directory]

User name: kasino72-1092351

Password: ********   ☑ Save Password

[OK] [Cancel] [Help]

46

If the Site Manager isn't already on screen, press F9 to display it. If your site contains any files or folders you'll see them in this panel, and you can use the icons to delete files, create new folders or rename files. First, though, we need to put some pages there. Find a page you want to publish and then click the Publish button in the main toolbar.

▾ **Nvu Site Manager**

View: [All files ▾]

[Edit sites]

Name
My web site

47

Nvu will now display the publishing settings for your page. Make sure "Include Images and other files" is ticked, and that "Use same location as page" is also ticked. The way we've put our site together means that all the pages and images need to be in the same folder: if they aren't, your site won't work properly.

Publish Page ✕

[Publish] [Settings]

Site Name: [My web site ▾] [New Site]

Page Title: Bigmouth strikes again: Music   e.g.: "My Web Page"

Filename: music.html   e.g,: "mypage.html"

Site subdirectory for this page:
[▾]

☑ Include images and other files
  ⦿ Use same location as page
  ○ Use this site subdirectory:
    [▾]

[Publish] [Cancel] [Help]

48

Click Publish and Nvu will now display the dialog shown in our screenshot. If there are any errors – such as a mistyped password – you'll see them here. If everything's working okay, then Nvu will tell you that the publishing process has been successful. If the progress bars don't seem to be doing anything, make sure you don't have firewall software or other security software that's preventing Nvu from accessing the internet.

49

If you click on the Refresh button (the yellow arrow) Nvu should now show the contents of your site. So far we've just uploaded a single page, but we can now go on and publish the rest of our site in exactly the same way as we published our music page.

50

Your pages are available to other internet users as soon as they've finished uploading. As you can see from our screenshot, the site works fine in Internet Explorer. It's a very good idea to click every link and look at every page before letting anyone know your site's address: at the bottom of this page we've forgotten to strip out some sample text!

PART **3** **Blogging on**

Websites made simple

Until recently, if you wanted to be a cool net user you needed to have a website. That's changed, and the really trendy techie types now boast about their "blogs". So what on earth is a blog and why should you care?

Blog is short for "weblog" and it's a term used to describe a website that's a cross between a personal diary and a collection of links. Using tools such as Blogger or Movable Type, thousands of people run their own blogs, talking about anything from pets to peace. There are celebrity blogs and political blogs, comedy blogs and carers' blogs, British blogs and Bulgarian blogs; there are right-wing blogs and left-wing blogs, teenage blogs and technical blogs. There's no doubt that blogs are becoming a big deal, and it's never been easier to build your own.

Blogs have actually been around for some time, although the term "blog" wasn't coined until the late 1990s. One of the first sites on the World Wide Web, Yahoo.com, could be described as a blog: these days it's a giant search engine, but in its infancy Yahoo! was just a list of interesting things people had found on the internet. People have been publishing online diaries since the internet was in short pants (they called it "journaling"), and lots of websites feature splenetic rants about the authors' pet subjects. What turned these different kinds of sites into blogs was the arrival of dedicated blogging tools such as Blogger, which makes publishing on the internet as easy as writing an email.

The search engine Google now indexes blogs as well as traditional websites. Check it out at **http://google.com/blogsearch** and you'll soon get the flavour of what makes a blog different...

Blogs vs websites

Technically blogs *are* websites. After all, they sit on the web and they're written in the same language as other web pages. However, there are a few key differences between blogs and more traditional websites.

The biggest difference between blogs and websites is that blogs work backwards. Where a normal website starts with an introduction, blogs start with the most recent thing you've written, followed by the next most recent thing and so on. In many cases the "hi, and welcome to my blog" page is buried in a remote corner of the blog – something that would be unthinkable in a normal site.

Another key difference is that blogs are very informal and unstructured. A website tends to be organised into sections, so for example you might have an "about me" page, a news page, a links page and so on. Blogs don't usually bother with all of that. Instead, everything is chucked onto the page as the author thinks of it, so it's not unusual to see a blog page that starts off talking about the political situation in the Middle East, includes photos of the author's cats and then recounts the gory details of a visit to the dentist. A blog entry might be a single sentence, or it could be a photograph; it could be a concert review, or an angry rant about Council Tax. That can be bad as well as good, as finding things on some blogs can be very difficult – especially if you're not too sure what you're looking for in the first place.

Blogs are almost always updated live on the internet, whereas traditional sites are generally built offline and then uploaded *en masse* at the end of the project.

Finally, blogs tend to be more interactive than websites. Most blogs enable you to add your own comments to the text, and other people can then comment on your comments. The author might respond, which in turn sparks off more comments, and before you know it there are dozens of people having a debate. Although you do find commenting systems on some websites (and there are plenty of blogs that don't have commenting systems), blogs are more conversational and tend to thrive on feedback from visitors.

A good example of the difference between a site and a blog is the *Guardian* newspaper site, which makes good use of blogs. On the site proper you'll find traditional news stories, but the site also includes a number of blogs where the newspaper's journalists can be more informal and get chatting with the readers.

In the *Guardian* newspaper and on the main *Guardian* site, stories are written in neutral language and have been fact-checked. In other words, they're good old-fashioned news articles. However, over on the *Guardian* blogs you'll find writers saying to the readers, "I think this is daft. What do you think?" or "We've no idea what's happening yet, but I hope that the Prime Minister sees sense on this one." The articles are proper journalism, while the blogs are a conversation.

In addition to its traditional news stories, the *Guardian* newspaper publishes a range of blogs where its writers can be less formal and vent their spleens.

The famous five

There's no such thing as a standard blog, as you'll discover when you look at five of the better-known blogs: Robot Wisdom, Scaryduck, Boing Boing, MetaFilter and Waxy.

Robot Wisdom (www.robotwisdom.com)

Robot Wisdom is one of the internet's most famous blogs and it follows a simple formula: every day Jorn Barger posts a big list of links with a very short explanation of what each one is. For example, a typical link might say "Wal-Mart drops local paper after too-honest report". If you want to know the full story, you'll need to click on the link. Robot Wisdom is blogging at its most minimalist.

Robot Wisdom is blogging at its most basic: a collection of links with a very short description of each one.

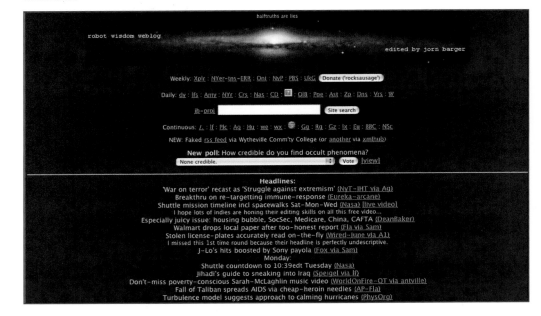

Scaryduck (http://scaryduck.blogspot.com)

Scaryduck is a good example of the blog as an online diary, and describes itself as "being in the main an account of the interesting and varied life of Scaryduck: genius, gentleman explorer, French cabaret chantoose [sic] and small bets placed". It's a very British blog, with regular updates on the author's adventures interspersed with the odd rant and lots of humour.

Scaryduck is a very British blog, with self-deprecating humour and the odd rant about life's little irritations.

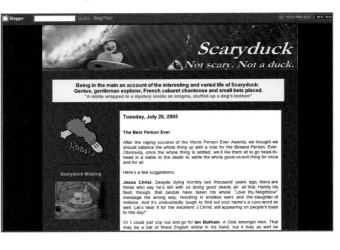

Boing Boing (www.boingboing.net)

Run by a handful of tech journalists, Boing Boing bills itself as "a directory of wonderful things" and provides links to the more interesting, worrying or plain weird stories on other sites. Unusually for a blog you can't add your own comments, although the site does solicit emails from readers and lists what other bloggers have to say about each story.

Boing Boing is good at finding the wackier side of technology, although some of its content is a little geeky for our tastes.

Waxy.org (www.waxy.org)

Andy Baio's blog covers technology and pop culture in a clever way. While the main blog consists of longish articles, there's also a sidebar at the right of the screen that provides links with a few words of commentary, Robot Wisdom-style. It's a good way of blogging about lots of different things without intimidating readers or giving them sore eyes.

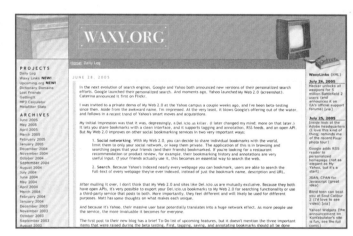

Waxy.org manages to combine long articles with lots of links in a way that won't give you a splitting headache.

MetaFilter (www.metafilter.com)

Most blogs are written by one person, or by a small group of people. MetaFilter, on the other hand, is put together by 25,418 – and rising – members. It covers every conceivable subject and it's one of our favourite weblogs.

MetaFilter works because of its clever structure. Stories on the front page are single paragraph affairs, and each one links to a dedicated page where MeFites (the users of MetaFilter) discuss the story. The blog is broken into sections, so there's AskMe for general questions ("How do I get red wine out of carpet stains?" "What's the best way to quit smoking?"), MetaTalk for discussions about the nuts and bolts of MetaFilter itself, and the main MetaFilter site for newsworthy and interesting things. Members are expected to follow some simple rules: don't post things we've all seen before, don't indulge in blatant self-promotion, and don't simply regurgitate things you've seen elsewhere on the internet. Because most people do follow these rules, MetaFilter's always worth reading.

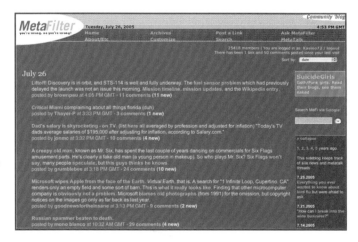

With 25,418 members, MetaFilter is one of the biggest and best community weblogs on the internet.

Building a blog

The popularity of blogs means that there's no shortage of excellent blogging tools to choose from. There are two main types: beginner-friendly packages that cover the essentials; and all-singing, all-dancing systems for professional publishing. Services such as Blogger are firmly in the first category, while advanced publishing packages such as Movable Type and WordPress are aimed at expert users.

The famous blogs we mentioned earlier use a variety of tools to get their message across. Scaryduck uses Blogger, which copes admirably with lots of visitors; the more techy Waxy.org is powered by the Movable Type system, which offers an incredible amount of control over every aspect of the site.

Which is best for you? If you're new to blogging, we'd recommend Blogger (**www.blogger.com**). Movable Type is more powerful, particularly if you want to organise your blog entries into categories or configure every single aspect of your weblog, but it costs money (from around £35 for non-commercial use) and requires some technical knowledge to get up and running. There's nothing to stop you from beginning to blog with Blogger and then buying Movable Type (**www.movabletype.org**) when your blog becomes more popular.

Blogging tools prove that sometimes the best things in life really *are* free. Blogger is excellent, and provides everything you need including professionally designed templates, lots of free web space and software that runs in your web browser to make publishing utterly painless. For most bloggers, Blogger is ideal – which is why we've chosen it as the subject of our next workshop.

Movable Type is a very powerful blogging tool but it costs money – if you're starting out, Blogger is a better and cheaper way to begin.

PART 3 Making your blog count

Whether you're creating a brand new blog or looking for ways of improving one you've already started, you can learn a lot from the other blogs on the web. From the good ones you'll learn the importance of being original, writing regularly, expressing yourself clearly and finding interesting topics to post about. From the bad, you'll learn to avoid sloppy writing, inconsistency of tone and failing to respect other bloggers and potential readers.

You should also heed the advice of successful bloggers, many of whom reveal their own tips and tricks through their blogs. If there's one thing bloggers like writing about more than their chosen theme, it's their blogs. But don't take anything you discover by reading other people's blogs, or anything you read in the rest of this chapter, as fixed and unbending. In the end there are no rules. The really successful blog is not the one with the punchiest writing, fanciest presentation and hottest news; it's the one that readers keep coming back to. If you can click with your readers, they'll keep you on the right track through their feedback and personal contributions.

What should your blog be about?

For some, the subject of their blog chooses itself. It's an issue they care deeply about and they want to share their opinions and ideas with a wider public. You'll find blogs concentrating on

Who would have thought the notion of recording the 14 miles of above-ground scenery on the route of London's Circle Line would result in an award-winning blog, especially as the photos are taken with a primitive pinhole camera: **www.nyclondon/blog**.

previous post   next post
Black and White Photography - Pinhole
tags: pinhole, london, polaroid 55, underground
Walking the Circle Line: Temple to Embankment

I am continuing my walk above London Underground's 27-stop 14-mile long Cirde Line. Trying to stay as directly above the line as I can manage, along the way I've been taking large format photographs with a primitive pinhole camera.

Previous installments: Barbican to Moorgate, Moorgate to Tower Hill, Tower Hill to Blackfriars, Blackfriars to Temple.

In this installment, I walked the short distance from Temple to Embankment.

Welcome
This weblog is a place for me to share my black and white photography as I produce it, share interesting websites as I come across them, and publish other news of photographic interest.

QE2 & Queen Mary 2
Competitive discounts on both the QE2 & Queen Mary 2
Ads by Goooooogle

Archives
Browse all previous posts 2001-2005

Categories
Black and White Photography
Black and White Photography - Pinhole
SX-70 Polaroid Manipulations
Equipment Reviews

Popular tags
pinhole
new york
london
street
leica
protest

My photo galleries
NYCLONDON.COM
- Street Photography
- Night Photography
- Portraits of Dissent
- Winter in New York
- Central Park
- Grand Central
- World Trade Center
- Polaroid SX-70

Articles
Polaroid SX-70 Manipulations

Neil Gaiman, hard-working novelist and comic book author, is a shameless self-publicist who writes almost exclusively about himself yet has one of the most frequented blogs on the web. Don't try this yourself unless you're already famous: **www.neilgaiman.com**.

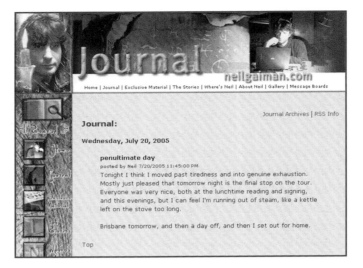

serious issues such as terrorism, poverty and human rights, but there are just as many covering personal, but still deeply felt, obsessions such as soaps and celebrities, rock climbing and rock music.

At the other end of the scale there are blogs designed solely to give the author a form of self-expression, and where there is no cohesive theme other than the author's desire to communicate about anything and everything. Blogs like these can be riveting if you have the time and talent to nurture them; but unless you're already famous for doing something else, it's unlikely you'll draw many readers to a personal site even if it's brilliantly written.

Between the two extremes, people write blogs for all sorts of reasons. Some do it to keep in touch with family and friends around the world, and others as a way of supplementing their income by including pay-per-click advertisements. Commercial organisations use blogs to promote their products, charities use them to promote their causes and writers use them to sell their books. Blogs are also written to make friends, to while away the time, to keep minds active, to learn about computers and to practise writing skills.

Personal and public blogs

Whatever it is that's inspiring you to create a blog will almost certainly help you pick a suitable subject to write about. If the blog is primarily intended for friends and family then the subject matter will be you, your loved ones, your jobs, home, pets, holidays and pastimes, and it doesn't really matter how well you write because your audience just wants to keep in touch. However, don't expect anybody who stumbles across your blog to come back in a hurry, even if your children are budding geniuses, your dog can walk on its hind legs and you've just been promoted at work.

If your blog is a mercenary attempt to generate income through pay-per-click advertising, the theme must be related to the advertising you intend to carry. The same holds true for commercial sites too. It's no good creating a fascinating blog about the rock music scene if your product is hand-made cheeses. Then again, neither would you want to limit yourself to cheese-making as a topic. Cheese-making doesn't change much from day to day and wouldn't benefit from the journal-style blog approach, so a blog focussing on healthy eating, gourmet recipes

How do you turn a company blog promoting a sheet metal-working concern in the wilds of Lancashire into an award-winning blog? Find out at **www.butlersheetmetal.com/tinbasherblog**.

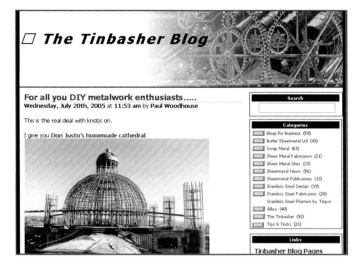

or modern lifestyles would be more suitable. It would also be easier to maintain because there's no shortage of constantly updated links on these topics.

Even better from a marketing point of view would be a blog called Hard Cheese, which could regale its readers with strange tales of coincidence and ill-luck, and be written with tongue firmly in cheek. It has the potential to attract a wider range of readers than a food-related site, and is the sort of subject likely to generate its own material thanks to readers' contributions.

A long-term endeavour

Whatever subject you decide to hang your blog around, make sure it's something that will maintain your interest and that of its potential visitors. Ideally you'll be updating it every day, so it's important to remain enthusiastic about the topic, especially as it takes a long time to build an interesting archive of past articles and posts that will serve as a bedrock for the daily journal entries. While you may yearn to own a blog that hits the news and becomes an overnight success, such sites are rare and they're nearly always tied to major news stories such as wars, scandals and crimes. Keeping a topical site going when interest in the subject starts to wane could turn into a very hard slog.

Boing Boing (**http://boingboing.net**) is a collaborative blog calling itself a directory of wonderful things, e.g. lingerie for cows and rugs patterned like giant slices of salami. Sites like these thrive because of the active participation of their readers.

Keeping your blog up to date

Once you know what you're going to write about you need to keep in touch with what's in the news and what people are talking about in your chosen field. Regardless of how cleverly your blog page is put together and how many fancy features and tricks it incorporates, what keeps readers coming back are the links you find to other sites and the comments you make about how you see the world.

Really Simple Syndication

Obviously, it's impossible to keep up to date by idly browsing the web because it's such a big place that you might easily miss stories of great interest. With almost every kind of print and broadcast media also directing much of its output to the web you need some way of cutting through the mountains of media fluff to locate items genuinely relevant to your blog. The primary technique is the use of RSS feeds. RSS stands for Really Simple Syndication and is a way of having updates from websites you're interested in delivered to your computer without you having to visit the site and trawl through stuff you've seen before. Not every site offers RSS feeds but those that do include all the major news gathering organisations including CNN and the BBC, plus

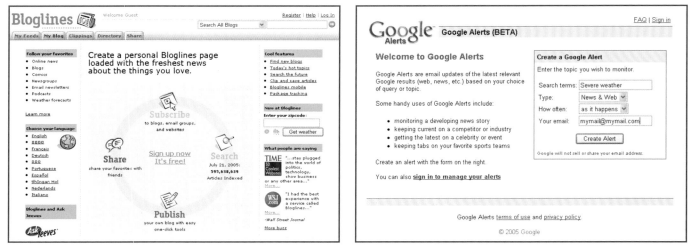

Bloglines (**www.bloglines.com**) is an online treasure chest for bloggers. You can build a blog, search other blogs and handle RSS feeds all from the same site.

The great thing about Google Alerts (**www.googlealert.com**) is that you don't have to join anything. Simply provide a valid email address to which search results can be sent.

leading world newspapers and magazines. In addition, there are RSS feeds from other blogs and from websites like How Stuff Works.

Subscriptions to RSS feeds are free, as is most of the software you need to read them. Technically such programs are called aggregators but they are commonly referred to as feeders or readers. You can choose between an RSS reader that displays your chosen feeds on a dedicated web page that you visit or one that runs on your PC as a stand-alone program. If you use a web browser such as Firefox or Opera (but not Internet Explorer), you can even read RSS feeds in your browser without having to go to a special web page.

News delivered to your inbox

Another way of keeping up to date is to register your email address with websites that send news, information and updates directly to your inbox. Not all websites offer this kind of service but many of them do. For sites that don't, you can use Google Alerts instead. A Google Alert is a pre-defined Google search, the results of which are emailed to you on a regular basis. You can choose to receive Google Alerts weekly, daily or as they happen. When you receive an Alert it contains clickable links you can follow, just like the results of an interactive Google search.

Two other services that that will keep your inbox supplied with regularly updated and relevant material are the special interest groups operated by Yahoo and Google. These groups, which offer a web-based alternative to the unregulated world of Usenet news groups, can be browsed online or you can have group updates sent to you by email, either as daily digests or when new posts are made. There are millions of Yahoo groups to choose from, and even though many of them are almost inactive there's a healthy number that are both on-topic and thriving. Google has almost 300,000 groups of which 3,000 are classified as highly active.

Three ways of handling RSS feeds

In the following step-by-step guides, you'll learn different ways of subscribing to RSS feeds so you can keep up to date with what's happening on selected websites and in other people's blogs. The first workshop describes the use of a dedicated RSS reader working independently of a web browser. The second demonstrates how to use an online service (in this case Newsgator) to locate and read RSS feeds. The third shows how Opera (**www.opera.com**), one of the alternative browsers to Internet Explorer, can view RSS feeds by treating them just like any other message.

Setting up and using FeedReader

1

*There are plenty of dedicated RSS readers to choose from. This workshop uses one called FeedReader. Being open source software, it's completely free and, at only 1.5MB, it takes less than five minutes to download even on a slower dial-up connection. Go to **www.feedreader.com** to get the latest version.*

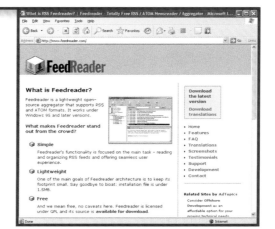

2

Double click on the downloaded file to install it. After installation FeedReader launches itself automatically. Around 20 feeds are pre-installed so you can start using it straight away. In the left-hand pane, double click on the News category to view all the headlines available from all the News feeds, and then click on BBC News to limit the display of headlines to only those from the BBC.

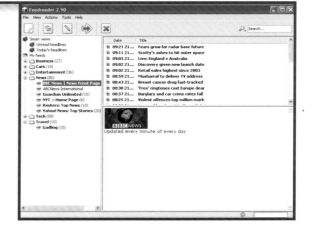

3

Click any of the headlines in the top right-hand pane and you'll see a summary of the selected article in the lower right-hand pane. To view the entire article click Read On. While you're doing this, don't be surprised to see pop-up messages in the lower right-hand corner of the screen announcing additional headlines as the BBC makes them available. To expand a news story to fill the FeedReader window use the F11 key, which invokes so-called Aquarium view. To return to normal view, simply press F11 again.

4

To add a new RSS feed to FeedReader, go to the web page of the site you want to add and look for an XML or RSS button (you'll find one at the bottom of the page at **www.telegraph.co.uk**). When you click the button it takes you to a page listing all the feeds available. Tick the box to show you accept the terms and conditions, and then click the UK News button.

5

This is the code that FeedReader or any other RSS reader can use to display UK news headlines from the Daily Telegraph, but the only part you need to concern yourself with is the URL at the top. Select this and press Ctrl+C to copy it to the Windows clipboard.

6

Switch to FeedReader and open the File menu, then click Add Feed. In the Add new feed dialogue box press Ctrl+V to paste the link you copied in step 5. Click Next. Select News as the folder where the feed should be created, and then click Finish. Feeds can be reorganised by dragging them into new folders, or deleted by right-clicking to select Delete current feed from the context menu.

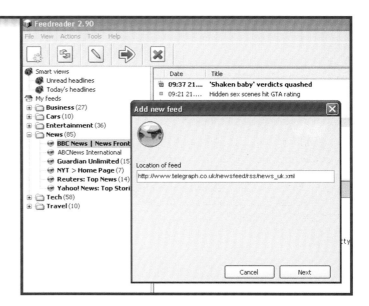

Using Newsgator to manage RSS feeds

Go to **www.newsgator.com** *and click on the "Sign up! It's Free!"*
button. Pick a user name and password, then provide a contact
name and email address. Click Next. Choose the type of
subscription you require (the free standard subscription is
selected by default) and then click Next. On the screen shown
here you can choose a selection of feeds to get you started.

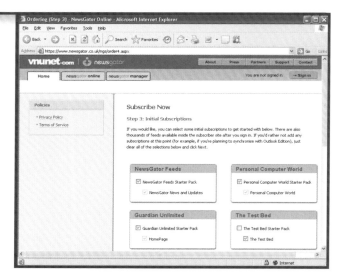

Click Next and your subscription is activated. Follow the
instructions and sign in using the details you've just provided,
then click the Newsgator Online tab. The feeds you chose when
subscribing are listed on the left of the screen. The bracketed
number after each feed indicates the number of stories it
contains. Click on any of the feeds to see its headlines and
summaries listed on the right of the screen.

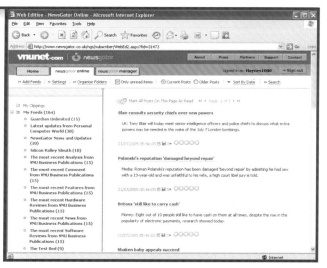

Click on any headline to display the web page containing the
story. To return to Newsgator use the Back button on your
browser. If you're using Internet Explorer's default settings you
might prefer to right click on a Newsgator headline and select
Open in New Window. In this way you can keep a story on
screen while pursuing new links in Newsgator.

4

You can add new feeds in several ways. If you've copied the URL of an RSS feed from a website (see steps 4 and 5 in the previous workshop), you can add it to Newsgator by clicking *Add Feeds* and then selecting the *URL & Import* tab. Paste the URL (in this case for the *Daily Telegraph's* motoring news) into the *Feed* panel and click the *Add Feed* button. Click the *Newsgator Online* tab to return to what you were doing.

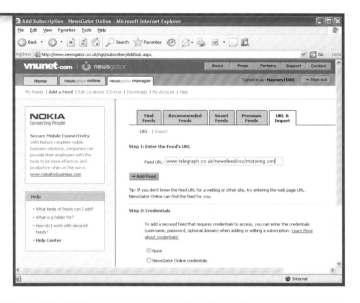

5

When you don't already have a URL the easiest way of adding new feeds is to use Newsgator's built-in search engine. Click *Add Feeds* and then select the *Find Feeds* tab. You may then browse through a categorised list of topics or find feeds by entering a search term. After searching you can click on the name of a site to view the site itself, or click on *Subscribe* to add the site's feed to your list.

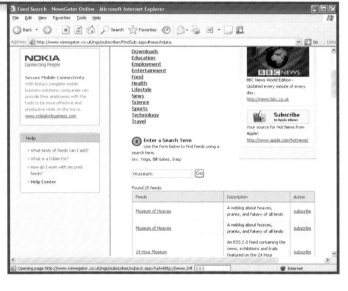

6

To remove feeds you no longer require, click on the *Newsgator Manager* tab and select the feeds, then click *Delete*. You will be asked to confirm the deletion. On the same screen you can organise feeds into folders instead of having them all lumped together. Simply tick the feeds to be grouped and then select *New Folder* in the *Move to Folder* list. After you click the *Move* button you will be prompted to name the new folder.

Using the Opera browser as a news feed reader

1

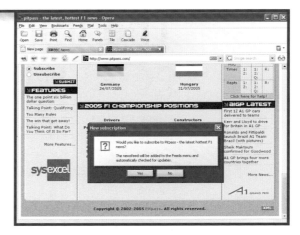

Here's how to add a news feed to Opera using an RSS or XML button displayed on a web page. Go to **www.pitpass.com** *and scroll down to the bottom of the page. Click on the XML button. When a pop up message asks you if you wish to subscribe, click Yes. The display will almost immediately change to Opera's email-style view showing PitPass headlines in the top pane. Click on any of these to view a link to the full story in the lower pane.*

2

To add a news feed to Opera when you already know the URL of the feed, open Opera's Feeds menu and select Manage Feeds. Click New and type (or paste) the URL into the Address panel. If you want to personalise the name of the feed, remove the tick against "Get name from feed" and type a new one into the Name panel. Use the drop-down list to choose how frequently you want to receive updates, then click OK.

3

You can delete feeds and set other options by clicking Manage Feeds on the Feeds menu. By removing the tick from a feed you suppress its display on the Feeds menu without actually deleting it. To permanently remove a feed, click to select the feed and then press the Delete button.

4

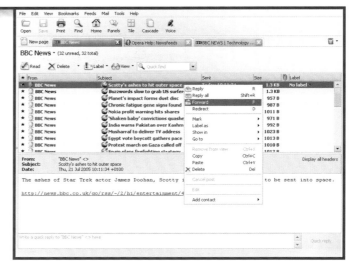

To change the name of a feed or the frequency with which you receive updates from it, select the feed and click Edit. This displays the properties of the link (as in step 2), which can be modified. If you use Opera as your email client, it's also possible to forward headlines and links to others who may be interested. Simply right click on an item in the top pane, select Forward, then type the recipient's address and click Send.

BLOGGING ON

The importance of good writing

A blog with badly-written and ungrammatical posts full of spelling mistakes is unlikely to attract return visitors. Even if you don't ascribe much importance to formally correct English when sending texts and emails, you should pull out all the stops when writing your blog. Establishing credibility is the primary goal of all aspiring bloggers, and if your writing suggests you don't care about language (or worse still that you can't even recognise good English) your blog will be dead in the water.

Unfortunately, on most of the popular sites where blogs are hosted, including the big ones like Blogger (**www.blogger.com**) and Bloglines (**www.bloglines.com**), there are no editing tools to help you write well. At Bloggit (**www.bloggit.net**), an assistant mimicking one of Microsoft's Office Assistants is superimposed on blog postings to point out any obvious mistakes the writer has made, but being corrected in public by a cartoon paperclip strikes us as a poor alternative to getting it right first time.

You can avoid public humiliation by editing your post in a decent word processor and then running its spelling checker (and, optionally, its grammar and style checkers) before copying and pasting the results into your blog. You don't have to act on the grammar and style advice, especially if you're aiming for an informal, punchy approach, but be sure to correct all the spelling mistakes.

Don't worry if you've never done any creative writing before: the more often you write, the easier it becomes. You can take the following tips on blog-writing style to heart or you can ignore them completely: after all, if what you have to say is fascinating

Mark Bernstein thinks most readers will forgive punctuation and spelling mistakes. Check out the rest of his advice on writing for the web at **www.alistapart.com/articles/ writeliving**.

This sort of post might amuse close friends but is unlikely to bring the casual reader back for more. To spare her blushes, there's no URL for this one.

WEDNESDAY, JULY 13, 2005

wednesday woes.

sigh. just recieved the cc bills and the amount is slightly more than expected. it just went up to an amount i could jolly well get a speedy 25 (not that i like to have 1). seriously, i didn't buy much over at taiwan. i merely went crazy over the blings and shoes (i bought a good n cheap 10 pairs back!). that's all. hongkees have better taste. sigh, there goes my ikea white side table and the matching vanity table plus the lv le cherry pochette. i dare not go on because it will reflect how many lemmings i actually have. bad, very bad.

anyhoos, 3 more days people. at least, i get to enjoy good food, fab company and kickass musik!

Stuart Hughes, BBC journalist and prize-winning blogger, demonstrates the power of short sentences. Check out his style at **http://stuarthughes.blogspot.com**.

Wednesday, July 13, 2005

"It is to the shame of the international community that this evil took place under our noses, and we did nothing like enough." Jack Straw, Srebrenica, 11th July

Now I'm back here in London, it seems almost surreal to think that just 24 hours ago I was in Srebrenica.

It's tempting to think that the atrocities committed there ten years ago happened in some far off land.

But Bosnia is just a short three-hour plane journey from the UK, right on Europe's doorstep.

Visiting Srebrenica was a deeply depressing experience -- one from which it's difficult to find any glimmers of hope.

Srebrenica is a town filled with ghosts.

The place is haunted by the memories of what happened there in 1995.

and relevant it will find an audience no matter how you choose to express it.

- Write as if you were composing a letter to a close friend, not writing the leader column of a national newspaper.
- Short sentences are good. They're easy to write and easy to follow. Short sentences don't need punctuation marks.
- Try to develop your own style, not copy somebody else's. When regular readers get to know your style they'll return for more of it, and they won't expect it to chop and change.
- Don't be afraid to use everyday language – it makes your blog more personal – but avoid local slang and colloquialisms. Your blog should be understandable by English speakers all over the world, not just in your own country.
- Reread every sentence you write and try to write it more clearly. Take out any words that don't add to the meaning.
- If you feel strongly about something, don't hold back, but don't let your blog turn into a rant. Tell your readers why you feel the way you do and why the subject is important.
- Don't use multiple exclamation marks. In fact, don't use them at all if you can help it.
- Don't write everything in capital letters. It's ugly and hard to read, and it's a real turn-off for many readers.
- Be consistent about the circumstances in which you use capital letters, italics, bold text and underlining. If you don't know why you're using a typographical effect, how will your readers?
- No punctuation is better than bad punctuation – so if in doubt, leave it out. Having said that, you owe it to your readers to find out what an apostrophe is and when to use it.

Almost any blog can be improved if its writer checks out the free online version of William Strunk's Elements of Style (**www.bartleby.com/141**), which is full of practical examples.

PART 3

20 tips for a successful blog

A blog becomes successful by being:

- Mentioned and linked to in other blogs
- Chosen as a site of the day by a blog host
- Found by popular search engines
- Recommended by word of mouth
- Given an award of some kind
- Picked up by the mainstream media

The chances of these things happening depend on how closely you follow the unwritten rules of blogging. Nobody will link to your blog unless you've got something interesting to say and you say it well, but your blog must also show regard for blog etiquette, which is really just another way of saying you've got to respect both your readers and your fellow bloggers.

We've organised 20 tips into a list of dos and don'ts with a bonus at the end in the form of suggestions for what to do on days when you can't think of anything to blog about. The tips are in no particular order, and they're all aimed at turning your blog into one that people will enjoy reading and one that stays on the right side of the law. There's nothing in here about making money, marketing or getting your blog listed by the big search engines, but if this is what you're after you'll find plenty of stuff on the web. Start with a search on "Boosting Google rankings" and take it from there.

If you can't think of a catchy title for your blog, take a look through the top 100 blogs listed at **www.technorati.com**. Two titles in the current list are "Best Page in the Universe" and "Something Awful'.

Currently tracking 13.7 million sites and 1.3 billion links.   **Sign Up!**   Already a member?

Technorati™   Search   Tags   **Popular**   About   Help

News   Books   Movies   Top 100 Blogs

Popular Blogs

The biggest blogs in the blogosphere, as measured by links.

Sponsored Links

Blog the Shadow Web
Blog and Tag Any Web
Page Help Create the
Shadow Web
www.shadows.com

Business Blogging
Stop fooling with so-called
CRM. Create real customer
relationships.
www.cerado.com

Blogging Evolved
Elegant. Powerful.
Professional. The better
way to put a blog online
www.squarespace.com/

Try MSN Spaces
Create blogs and share
photos with your friends
on MSN Spaces
www.msnspacerace.co.uk

1 Boing Boing: A Directory of Wonderful Things
   15,770 links. View All »

2 Instapundit.com
   10,688 links. View All »

3 Daily Kos
   10,072 links. View All »

4 Gizmodo
   9,770 links. View All »

5 Drew Curtis' FARK.com
   9,674 links. View All »

Do:

- Give your blog a catchy and unique title, and preferably one that's at least obliquely relevant to the theme of your blog. People who like your blog will bookmark it, but they've got to find it first.
- Write to please an audience of one: yourself. Constantly ask yourself whether you'd still be reading your blog if somebody else had written it. If the answer is yes, you're a success.
- Compose your blog in easily-digestible chunks. Blog readers are browsers, and if they want to read long screeds of text they'll pick up a book. Keep sentences short, include bullet points and use descriptive headings to split up long sections.
- Post regularly. Every day is the target (some people post even more frequently) but if this isn't possible, aim for at least twice a week. One of British prime minister Harold Wilson's most enduring remarks is that a week is a long time in politics. In the blogosphere, it's even longer, and a blog with no activity for a week starts to drop off most people's radar screens.
- Include an email address in your blog but not your usual private one. Set up a separate address just for your blog. It's bound to attract a certain amount of spam even if you use spam-dodging tricks such as writing **mary@REMOVETHISuk.pippex.net**, but a separate email address can be changed as often as you like without affecting your regular email.
- Answer all polite emails sent by individuals in good faith. You can ignore the rest.
- Warn people if you provide a link to any web page or blog that contains material they may find offensive or disturbing. As a rule of thumb, this means anything you'd be shocked to see on the front page of a reputable newspaper.
- Credit other bloggers whenever you can. If you use a link you found in somebody else's blog, say where you got it, and whenever you mention a blogger by name it's good manners to include a link to their blog.
- Include relevant pictures in your blog. They add colour and break up the page. But don't go over the top because not everybody has a broadband connection. Always crop and resample pictures to achieve the smallest possible file size, providing a link to a higher resolution version of the picture where necessary.
- Tell people before you go on holiday or if for any other reason you will not be updating your blog for a while. If you expect readers to come back, announce the date on which you'll be resuming regular posts and stick to it come hell or high water.

Don't:

- Pass off speculation or opinion as fact. People are interested in your comments but you've got to make it clear when you're commenting and when you're reporting.
- Use misleading headlines in your posts. Headlines are likely to get picked up by search engines and readers get justifiably angry if they visit your blog after searching for information and find you writing about what you had for breakfast.
- Post when you are angry. If you're feeling passionate about something, write a blog entry by all means, but don't post it until you've calmed down and read it again.
- Attack other bloggers personally. By all means attack what they say, but only by providing reasoned arguments, not insults.

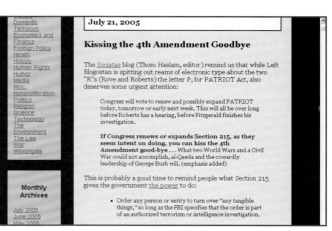

A good example of how splitting a complex article into chunks makes it easier for readers to find a way into it (**http://billmon.org**).

Flickr is not only a source of millions of free-to-use images, it incorporates a one-click "Blog This" option that adds pictures to your blog (**www.flickr.com**).

At **http://creativecommons.org** you can search for pictures, audio, video and literary works that you may freely add to your blog.

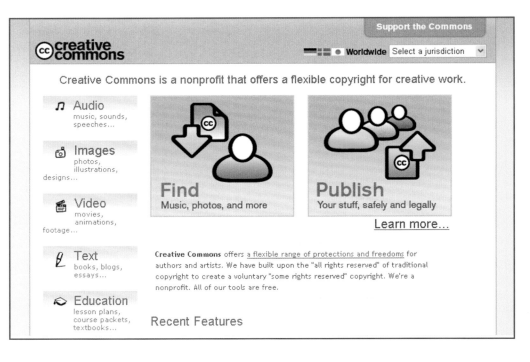

- Rewrite what other bloggers have said. Make a comment and attribution instead, always linking to the original article.
- Rewrite, edit or delete your old posts or archives. If you regret something you've previously posted, add a comment to this effect or make an apology. An inconsistent blog has no credibility and neither does its author.
- Lose potential readers by getting over-involved in cross-blog chatter. This may interest you but it's a turn-off for new visitors.
- Give out personal information about anybody (including email addresses and telephone numbers) – unless of course they've published this information themselves.
- Steal bandwidth from other bloggers by linking to pictures and multimedia material stored on their sites. Transfer files to your own server and link to them there.
- Use pictures to which you do not own the rights, especially if your blog has a commercial element. Remember that royalty-free does not mean payment-free, and don't assume you can use a picture just because it is included on a clip-art CD. Copying pictures from books and magazines is another no–no: just because you scan a picture doesn't make it yours. On the positive side you'll find plenty of pictures in the public domain or usable through a Creative Commons agreement at **www.flickr.com** and **http://creativecommons.org**. Whenever you publish a picture in your blog, regardless of its copyright status, remember to include an attribution saying where you got it and from whom.

What if there's nothing to write about?

Just as conventional print and broadcast media organisations have their silly seasons, there'll be times when nothing seems to be happening in connection with your blog, leaving you wondering what to write about. One approach is simply to skip making new entries until something catches your eye. After all, there's no law that says you have to blog every day. On the other hand, there are lots of things you can do to tide you over until things pick up.

One solution is to write about personal matters instead of sticking strictly to the theme of your blog. Your readers will probably be keen for an insight into your life when you're not blogging. Another possibility is to post a picture and talk about that, or skim through your online archives and find an existing post you can usefully update.

One of the things newspapers do on slow news days is to instigate a poll and publish the results. This usually involves interviewing a handful of passers-by on the street outside the office. You can do something similar by putting questions in your blog and asking your readers to contribute by email or through online comments, and publishing the results will give you something to write about on another day. In a similar vein you could write a post inviting your readers to comment on the blog itself, asking them whether you should change the screen template, find a new host, use more (or fewer) pictures, or whether they know any good sites you should add to your blogroll.

Perhaps one of the reasons you can't find anything new to write about is because you're always looking for news in the same places. Try widening your searches for on-topic news, or go to one of the popular websites like **www.snopes.com** (urban legends), **www.breakthechain.org** (e-mail scams and chain letters) or **www.darwinawards.com** (weird accidents) to find something that simply tickles your fancy, then comment on it.

At **www.newsisfree.com/newsmap**, the colour-coded map views of world news stories are a great way of putting yourself in touch with the current buzz.

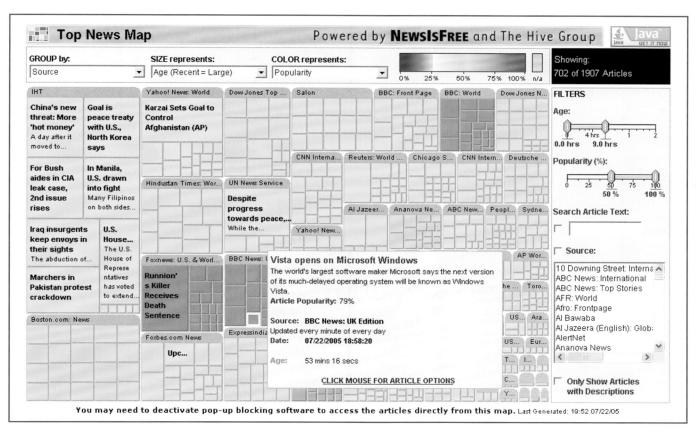

PART **4**

Building a blog with Blogger

Basic blogging

In this workshop, we'll build a weblog, or blog, using the excellent Blogger. The service is completely free and even includes web space. It's so easy to use that you can build a blog in a matter of minutes.

Although Blogger is simple, that doesn't mean it's basic. As we'll discover in this workshop, you can choose from a range of professional designs to give your pages real impact, you can use word-processor-style text formatting, and you can even enable visitors to leave comments on your blog.

One of the great things about Blogger is that it's ideal for beginners and experts alike. If you're new to the internet you'll find the whole process nice and easy, but if you're a bit more experienced you'll love the advanced tools that enable you to integrate your blog with an existing website or that let you tweak every conceivable part of your blog. There's also a range of free add-ons that can make your blog even more powerful.

First things first, though. Let's build a blog!

All you need to use Blogger is a web browser and an internet connection. It doesn't really matter which browser you use, although if you don't use Internet Explorer you'll find that some toolbars don't appear. We'll stick with Internet Explorer in this workshop. The first step is to visit **www.blogger.com** *to start the sign-up process.*

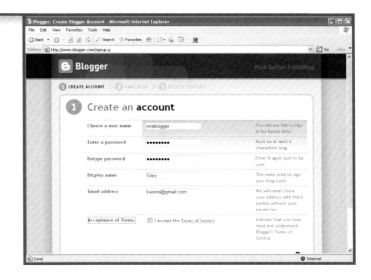

The first thing you'll need to do is to choose a user name. This will be part of your blog's internet address, so try to choose something memorable and snappy. You might find that you'll need to try a few options before your user name is accepted, because the most obvious names have been taken. In this screenshot we tried "imablogger" but it had already been used, so we went for "celeblogger" instead.

Once your name has been accepted, you'll need to give your blog a title. This will appear on every page of your blog, so it's worth spending a bit of time to come up with something snappy. Once you've done that, type the words you see on the screen (this is to prove you're not a software robot) and then click Continue.

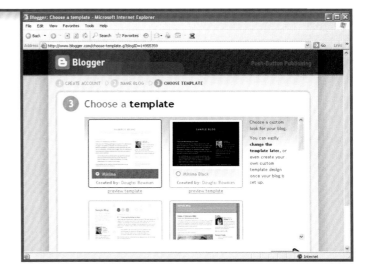

Blogger gives you lots of professionally designed templates to choose from, so scroll down until you see one you like and then select the check box for that template. Clicking on the Preview Template link opens the selected template in a new window. We'll use the Dots template for now – as we'll discover, it's easy to change the template later on.

5

Once you've found the template you want to use, scroll down and click Continue. And that's it! Blogger will now display the in-progress screen, which is a yellow triangle with a black exclamation mark. The wheel around the triangle will spin for a few seconds as Blogger stores your settings.

6

If everything's gone according to plan then you should see this screen, which tells you that your blog has been successfully created. For now, your blog is completely blank – so the next step is to add some content. Each article on a blog is called an "entry" or a "post", so let's start posting.

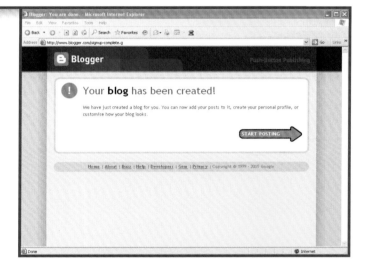

7

This is the main Blogger posting screen. Don't worry if the Title box doesn't appear in your browser window: not all templates use it, so if your chosen template is one of them then you won't see the Title box. No matter what template you used, though, you can start typing text in the main editing box, i.e. the big white bit in the middle of the screen.

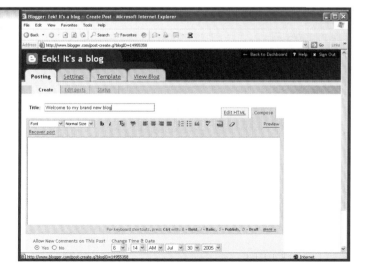

8

You can use the toolbar to jazz up your text by, for example, changing the font, making text bold or even changing the text colours. Try not to get too carried away, because the more text effects you use the harder your text will be to read. It's a good idea to stick with one font for your text and to use bold, italics or colours sparingly.

9

The toolbar includes a handy button called the Blockquote button, which has two inverted commas on it. You can use this to make quoted text stand out on your page. Simply highlight the text you want to use and click on the button, and Blogger turns it into a block quote. In the editing window the text will now appear indented. Some templates also use different colours for block quotes.

10

Click on the Preview link at the right of the toolbar to see how your blog entry will look. If you've used a title it will appear in bold at the top of the text, and the rest of your text will appear in the middle of the screen. Any formatting such as centred text, bold text or block quotes will also appear in the Preview. Click on Hide Preview to return to the editing window.

11

Underneath the main editing window you'll see two buttons: Save as Draft, and Publish Post. Save as Draft stores your post but doesn't put it on your blog, which is handy if you haven't got the time to finish an article. We're ready to roll, though, so click on Publish Post to share your thoughts with the whole world.

12

You may see the yellow in-progress triangle for a few seconds (once your blog becomes quite big, it'll appear whenever you publish new entries), but it's quickly replaced with the "success" page shown here. If there were any problems, Blogger will tell you about them now. However, everything's gone swimmingly so let's have a look at the results. Click on "(in a new window)" to see your first ever blog post.

13

Congratulations – you're now a blogger! As you can see, Blogger has combined your text with the template you chose to create a smart-looking page, and it has automatically added in some links. As you add more posts, Blogger automatically updates the "previous posts" section of the screen. You'll also see a line that says "0 comments". Click on this to see Blogger's comments system.

14

This is the comments screen, where anyone can add their tuppenceworth to your blog entry. Adding a comment is as simple as typing your text in the "Leave your comment" box and then clicking Login and Publish. As you're currently logged in to Blogger, you won't need to provide a password when you do this.

15

After a few seconds you should see your comment in the left-hand side of the screen. If other people add their comments, they'll appear below yours. Don't worry if, when you go back to your blog page, the link still says "0 comments", as it sometimes takes a few minutes for comments to appear live.

16

After a couple of minutes, anyone who visits your blog will now see a link that says "1 comments" instead of "0 comments". As you'd expect, this number increases with every new comment that gets added, and you'll soon find yourself checking out your own weblog to see whether anybody's added anything since your last visit. Close this browser window when you're ready to return to Blogger and make some more tweaks.

SUNDAY, JULY 31, 2005

This is where you type the actual text of your blog entry, and as you can see it's just like using a word processor. You use the toolbar to add **bold** or *italic*, to **change the fonts**, to format your text as bullet points or lists, and so on.

There are some handy other options too. If you want to quote someone else's text, you'd format it using the blockquote button (which looks like quote marks in the toolbar). It looks like this:

> Round and round the ragged rocks, the rugged rascal ran.

posted by Gary @ 2:42 AM   ● 1 comments

17

Blogger should still be open in your first browser window. In this step, we'll change the template to something a bit more professional-looking. To do this, click on the Template tab at the top of the screen and you should see Blogger's template screen, as shown in our illustration. Click on the "Pick New" link at the top left of the window.

18

Blogger will now display its entire template gallery. The templates are editable, too, so if you can't quite find what you need you can always choose a design that's similar to your needs and then tweak it yourself. If you see a small magnifying glass in the corner of a picture, you can click on it to display a much bigger version of that template.

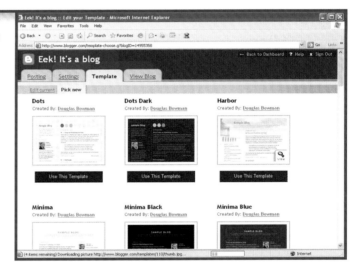

19

As you can see, there are lots of templates to choose from. We like the Rounders 3 template, which you'll find about halfway down the page: it uses a nice, clear colour scheme and works well on personal and business blogs alike. To choose the Rounders 3 template, click on "Use This Template" immediately below the template picture.

20

Blogger will now take you back to the Templates page. Although you've selected a new design, your blog hasn't been updated yet. To make your existing post follow the new template, you'll need to republish your blog. You'll see two options: Republish and Republish Index. The former republishes your entire blog, which can take time if you've been blogging for a while, and the latter only republishes the blog's front page.

21

Click on Republish and you'll see the in-progress screen for a few seconds. When the process is finished, Blogger will display the success page shown in our screenshot. To see the results, click the "(in a new window)" link to see your blog in a new browser window.

22

As you can see, Blogger has taken your existing weblog and completely changed the design. You should notice a few similarities – the comments have been transferred and your text formatting remains intact – and a few differences. For example, this template handles block quotes differently, so your block-quoted text will appear with dotted lines above and below it.

23

Click on the View My Complete Profile link to see your Blogger profile. Because you're logged in you can change the details, but don't worry: your visitors will only be able to read your profile and won't be given the opportunity to make changes. Use this screen to add any extra information such as where you are, what you do or what films, books and movies interest you.

24

Back in Blogger, you can use the Settings tab to make all kinds of changes to your blog. You can change the time zone, put limits on who can add comments, find out how to update your blog by email, and you can even build a team blog. This is a blog where you have multiple writers, and you can add friends or family to your blog team by using the Members section of the Settings screen.

If you don't like the way Blogger handles visitor comments you can get a free replacement system from Haloscan (**www.haloscan.com**). Similarly if you want to add lots of links, there's a free system called BlogRolling (**www.blogrolling.com**) that makes it easy to add your favourite sites to your weblog. In both cases it's just a matter of copying a few lines of text into your Blogger template.

PART 4

Better blogging

One of the golden rules about using the internet is that the more you can do, the more you want to do – and blogging is no exception. We've already looked at the basics of web publishing using Blogger but, in this workshop, we'll get stuck into some of Blogger's more advanced features. We'll find out how to publish photographs, how to replace the comments system with something a bit faster and more flexible, and we'll also look at a free add-on that enables you to share your favourite web links with your blog visitors.

We'll also look at two very clever bits of Blogger: team members and email. The former means that you can invite other people to contribute to your weblog. For example, you could have a "guest blogger" updating your blog when you're too busy to write anything or when you're away on holiday. If you can't bear to spend even a day without blogging, though, we'll discover how you can use Blogger's email features to update your blog from any email account – so if your mobile phone has an email program, you could post blog entries from the beach without going anywhere near a computer.

Although we're going to cover some of Blogger's more advanced features, don't worry: everything we'll look at is nice and simple to use, and even the most powerful options only require a couple of mouse clicks.

1

In Blogger Settings you'll find lots of options to help make your blog work exactly the way you want it to. In the Formatting section you can change the time zone, the way dates appear in your posts and even the language in which the dates should appear. You can also specify how many entries should appear on your blog's front page (the default is seven days).

2

If your blog doesn't include a title field but you'd like to use one, it's easy to add. Scroll to the bottom of the Formatting screen and change Show Title Field from "No" to "Yes". If you wish, you can also enter some HTML code in the Post Template field – this will then appear in the editing window whenever you create a new blog entry.

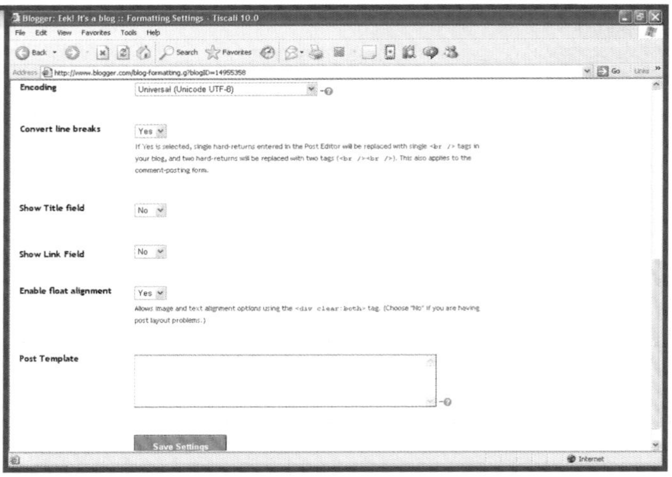

3

One of the more irritating things about the web is spam, but Blogger has a way to combat weblog spam. If your comments are full of rubbish trying to sell people things, go to the Comments tab and select "Yes" next to "Show Word Verification for Comments". This means visitors have to copy some on-screen text before their comments will be accepted, which stops automated spam systems from spoiling your blog.

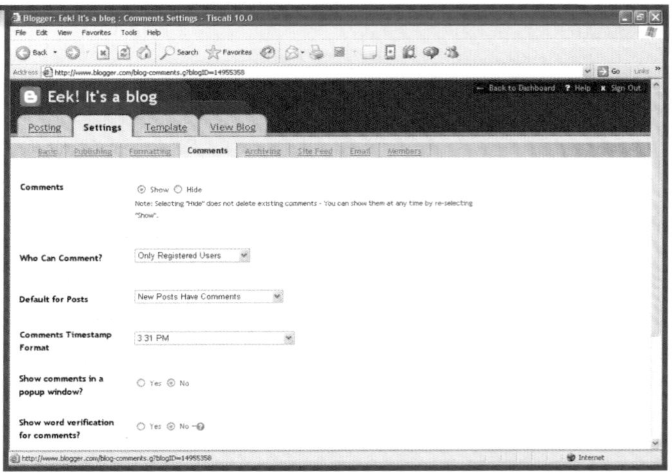

4

These days more and more people read weblogs using programs called RSS readers, which means it's a very good idea to publish a feed of your own. To do this, click on the Site Feed option and change Publish Site Feed to "Yes". You can then choose whether to provide all of your blog in your feed or just a short summary of each article.

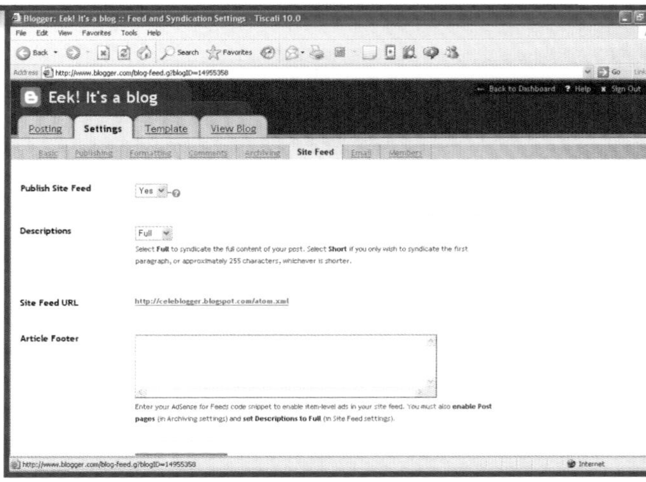

5

In the Email tab, you'll find something handy: blogging by email. This enables you to post to your blog when you don't have access to a web browser. Choose a secret word in the "Mail-To-Blogger-Address" and click Publish; this will be your super-secret blogging address. For example, if your secret word was "secret" then the email address would be **yourblogusername.secret@blogger.com***. Try to choose something a bit less obvious than "secret", though!*

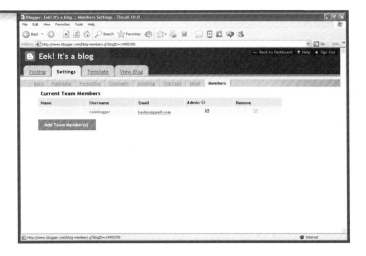

6

You can also make mobile blogging open to other people. To do this click on the Members tab and then on Add Team Member(s). Enter the email address of anyone you want to add to your blog and wait for them to accept or decline the invite. Once they've joined they can use the same email address to post to your weblog. It's worth remembering that any such posts will appear under your name.

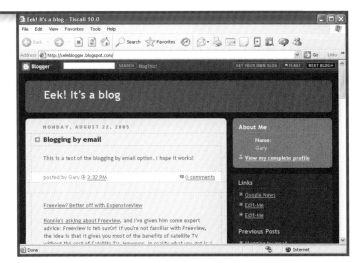

7

Once you've set up your secret blogging email address, you can create a new post wherever you can get access to email. Simply send an email to your secret blog address and Blogger will automatically publish it for you. The subject of your email will become the blog post headline and the content of your message will be the actual blog entry.

8

One of the easiest ways to spice up a weblog is to add photos, and Blogger makes it nice and simple to add images to your weblog. Store the photo somewhere handy – we use the Desktop – and then create a new post in Blogger. Once you've done this, click on the Image icon in the toolbar (it's the second icon from the right) to open Blogger's photo features.

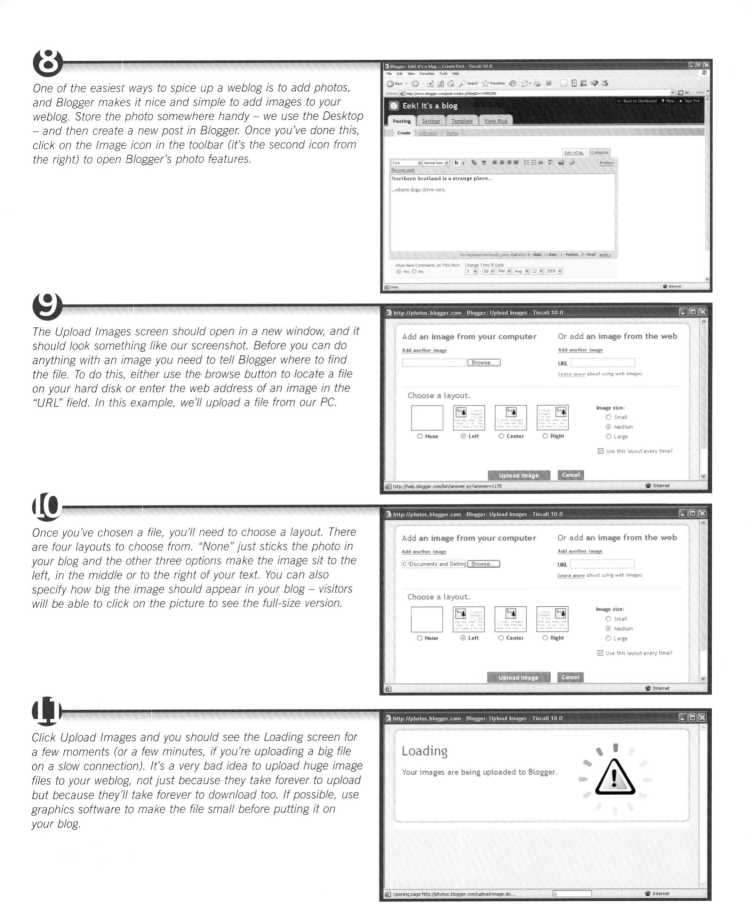

9

The Upload Images screen should open in a new window, and it should look something like our screenshot. Before you can do anything with an image you need to tell Blogger where to find the file. To do this, either use the browse button to locate a file on your hard disk or enter the web address of an image in the "URL" field. In this example, we'll upload a file from our PC.

10

Once you've chosen a file, you'll need to choose a layout. There are four layouts to choose from. "None" just sticks the photo in your blog and the other three options make the image sit to the left, in the middle or to the right of your text. You can also specify how big the image should appear in your blog – visitors will be able to click on the picture to see the full-size version.

11

Click Upload Images and you should see the Loading screen for a few moments (or a few minutes, if you're uploading a big file on a slow connection). It's a very bad idea to upload huge image files to your weblog, not just because they take forever to upload but because they'll take forever to download too. If possible, use graphics software to make the file small before putting it on your blog.

12

Whatever you do, don't close the window until you see this message: if you close the window too early, then any time spent uploading your image may have been wasted. Once the upload has been completed, click on Done and the window will close automatically. You'll now be returned to the main browser window.

13

You should now see your image in the editing window. If you chose a specific layout, the design on-screen should reflect that layout. In this example we chose the Left option, so our image appears on the left of the screen and our text is on the right. If everything looks OK, click Publish to add the finished result to your weblog.

14

Once the publishing process has completed, click View Blog and you should see something like this. We've chosen the middle image size, which means that some of the smaller details aren't too clear. However, the image is clickable, so if someone clicks on the picture Blogger will display the full-size version in all its glory.

15

On many weblogs you'll see a big list of links, called a "blogroll". Although it's possible to create such a list manually, it's very time consuming. A much better idea is to sign up with a free service such as **www.blogrolling.com**, which gives you a "Blogroll It!" button for your browser toolbar. When you see a site you'd like to add to your links list, simply click Blogroll It to add it to your blog. Easy!

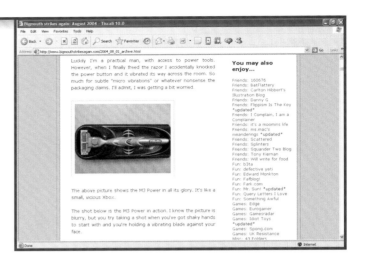

16

If you don't like Blogger's comments system, there are plenty of alternatives. We like Haloscan (**www.haloscan.com**) because it's very flexible and won't cost you a penny. To add the system to your site, you'll need to register with Haloscan. This can take a few minutes as you need to wait for a confirmation email before you can complete the registration process.

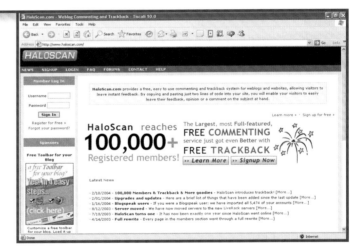

17

Once you've signed up for a Haloscan account and logged in, the next step is to choose the platform you want Haloscan to create the code for. Blogger is the default option, but if you decide to use a different blogging system at a later date you'll be able to use Haloscan with that system too. Make sure Blogger is the selected option and then click Next.

18

Haloscan now generates the necessary code for you to add to your weblog. It looks a bit technical but it's really straightforward: open your Blogger account in a new browser window and go to the Templates tab, and then follow Haloscan's instructions. Replacing Blogger's comments with the Haloscan system is just a matter of cutting and pasting from one window to the other.

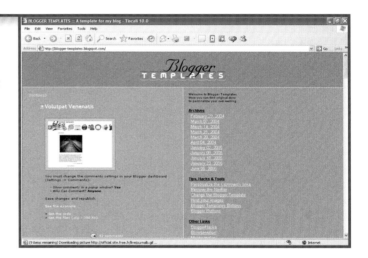

19

If Blogger's templates don't float your boat, there are plenty of sites offering free templates that you can use in your weblog. One of our favourites is Blogger Templates (**http://blogger-templates.blogspot.com**), which goes for quality over quantity: it might not have thousands of templates, but the ones it does feature are very smart indeed. The site also has a busy community so if there's a problem with a template, you'll often find the solution in the user comments.

20

Blogger regularly adds new features, and the best place to find out about them is on the Blogger Buzz site at **http://buzz.blogger.com**. Blogger Buzz is written by Blogger employees, but it's not just a place for announcements. The site also features insider information on how to get the best from blogging and explanations of any controversial new features. In our screenshot, Blogger Buzz explains how users can notify Blogger of potentially offensive content on people's weblogs.

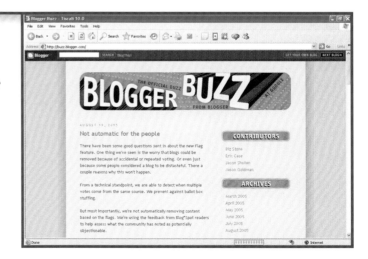

21

For now, Blogger's mobile phone service is US-only – but it's just a matter of time before it comes to the UK. When it does, you'll be able to start a new mobile blog by sending an MMS message to **go@blogger.com**. This sets up your mobile blog and sends you a claim code, which you can use to login to Blogger Mobile on the web. It's simple, fast and free.

22

One of Blogger's handiest features is also its simplest. Instead of using the mouse to do things, you can use keyboard shortcuts (if you're using Internet Explorer or the Firefox browser). For example, Control+B makes text Bold; Control+I makes it italic; Control+Z is undo and Control+Y is redo; Control+Shift+A is a link; and Control+S publishes your post. If you're a prolific blogger, these shortcuts will save you stacks of time.

Even better blogging

When you write a weblog it's a good idea to read lots of other people's blogs, too – partly because there's lots of good stuff out there, but more importantly to get ideas for your own blog.

When you read other people's blogs you'll spot all kinds of things. Some of them enable you to browse specific categories. For example, a blog about computers might have entries about Apple computers, entries about Microsoft software, entries about gadgets and entries about mobile phones. Many blogs enable you to see only those entries in a specific category, which makes life much easier if you're looking for something specific.

Another thing you'll see on many blogs is a little box containing Google adverts, which the site owner is using to (hopefully) generate money from their site. Other bloggers ask their readers for donations, either in cash or in the form of Amazon.co.uk wish lists; essentially they're saying, "if you like my blog, please buy me some stuff or give me some money". Amazingly, many readers do just that – particularly on the busiest blogs.

If you look at other blogs' comments, you might also see a section called "trackbacks", or headed "other blogs that link to this post". Here you'll find a list of links to other weblogs. A particularly controversial blog entry might be praised by some other bloggers and criticised by others. Elsewhere you might see "podcasts" – blogs in the form of audio files rather than on-screen text – or even "screencasts" or video blogs, which are the same thing but using video rather than audio.

What do all of these things have in common? None of these features are provided by Blogger – or at least, not by default.

Blogging for bucks

Can you make money from your blog? The short answer is probably no. Unless you're attracting millions of visitors, it's very unlikely that you'll be able to rake in stacks of cash. Unfortunately, most bloggers can only look with envy at blogging celebrities such as Andrew Sullivan (**www.andrewsullivan.com**), who regularly brings in five-figure sums by asking his readers to cough up some cash.

That doesn't mean you can't make any money, though. Putting some unobtrusive Google adverts on your site could generate the odd bit of pocket money, and it's free to set up. Simply head over to Blogger and log in, and then look at the right-hand panel (just below the profile information). You'll see a short bit of blurb suggesting that you should sign up for Google AdSense along with a link that takes you to the sign-up page.

Google AdSense is a simple and effective way to generate a bit of cash from your blog. When you sign up for the service – it's free – you'll be asked to choose from a gallery of different designs, and then Google automatically generates the appropriate code. Copy the code and paste it into the appropriate bit of your Blogger template (the AdSense pages give you full step-by-step instructions), and whenever you publish your blog Google will stick a couple of ads on it. Whenever someone clicks on an ad, Google counts the clicks and pays you a small sum. Don't expect to get rich quickly, though: the rate per click is often less than a penny, so you'll need to amass lots of clicks before there will be enough AdSense cash to transfer into your bank account.

AdSense is very clever. Whenever you publish a new blog entry, it scans your text and tries to find appropriate adverts – so for example if you blog about back pain, you're likely to see adverts offering various treatments for back pain. Unfortunately this can sometimes backfire, and you might find that your devastating exposé of medical frauds ends up displaying adverts for the very people you're telling your readers to avoid. The good news is that you can prevent such things from happening again by logging into your AdSense account and using the advertising filters to block most inappropriate adverts.

Cynics might think, "Aha! I can put the ads on my page and click them repeatedly myself!" That's a bad idea. Google is wise to such tricks and will quickly boot you out of the AdSense programme if it thinks you're trying to cheat the system. That doesn't mean you can't use the system to your advantage, though. The more obscure a topic, the more money advertisers are likely to pay for ads on that topic; so adverts about music are likely to have a very low per-click fee, whereas ads for specialist things will pay much more. One enterprising blogger realised this, did some research and set up a blog about the asbestos industry. He knew nothing about asbestos, but knew that asbestos-related advertising paid serious money.

Andrew Sullivan is one of the web's more famous bloggers, and regularly brings in five-figure sums by asking his readers for donations. Unfortunately most bloggers will be lucky to bring in more than pocket money!

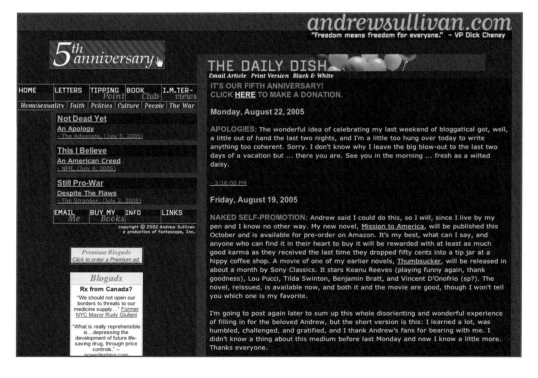

Make a wish

On many blogs you'll see a "donate!" button, often with the logo of the PayPal money transfer service. This enables your readers to donate cash via their debit or credit cards, which you can then transfer from your PayPal account to your bank. PayPal accounts are free (you can sign up at **www.PayPal.com**) but the service does take a cut of each transaction, usually a couple of pence.

Is it worth it? If you're expecting random strangers to turn up and give you cash then probably not. However, many bloggers find that occasional requests for donations can bring in a little bit of money for specific things, such as the cost of running their website. Adding a donation button to your blog won't do you any harm, but we wouldn't recommend that you should mention it at every opportunity. There's no better way to alienate your readers than to constantly beg for their money!

Another option is to create an Amazon Wish List. As the name suggests this is a list of things you'd like to buy from **www.Amazon.co.uk**, but which you haven't bought yet. Although the lists were originally designed for people to give their friends and family some big hints for Christmas and birthday presents, many bloggers have added wish lists to their blogs too. It's a "you scratch my back and I'll scratch yours approach": you provide a fascinating weblog and your readers buy you the odd book or DVD. To create a list, all you need to do is log in to Amazon and follow the on-screen instructions. This creates a wish list page to which you can then link from your weblog. As with donations, don't expect strangers to buy you lots of goodies, but once again it won't do any harm and you might get the odd pleasant surprise.

Many bloggers use **www.Amazon.co.uk** wish lists in an attempt to persuade their readers to buy them presents. It works, sometimes.

Podcasts such as the Tartan Podcast (**www.tartanpodcast.com**) include music donated by unsigned musicians.

Sound and vision

One of the things that's getting bloggers excited is podcasting, which uses blogging technology to deliver audio files rather than text. It's popular because your readers become listeners and, instead of reading your words on screen, they can listen to you on their iPods.

Although Blogger doesn't support podcasting as such, it's still possible to add podcasts to your blog – although you'll need your own web space to do it.

Creating a podcast is simple: just use a free recording program such as Audacity (**http://audacity.sourceforge.net**) to record your podcast, export the file as an MP3 and then stick it on the web. Adding the podcast to your blog is then just a matter of creating a new post and including a hyperlink to your MP3 file, such as **www.mywebspace.com/podcasts/myfirstpodcast.mp3**. Other blogging systems such as Movable Type can do this bit automatically, but we'll return to them in a moment.

There are two things you need to consider before podcasting (or three, if you include deciding what you want to talk about!). The first is music and the second is bandwidth. Getting either one wrong could prove expensive, so it's important to know the potential dangers.

It's illegal to use people's music without their permission. In the case of famous musicians, that permission takes the form of a licence from the Mechanical-Copyright Protection Society (**www.mcps.co.uk**), which will cost you a few hundred pounds per year. Without such a licence, you can't legally use other people's music and the penalties can be steep. One way to get around this is to find music by bands that haven't got a record deal. These bands – often called "unsigned bands" – are usually delighted to let you use their music and you won't need an MCPS licence to podcast their material.

Bandwidth means data transfer, and the bigger the file the more bandwidth each download will use. For example, 1MB of data is the equivalent of hundreds of pages of text – but a typical three-minute MP3 will be 3MB or 4MB in size. If your hosting firm has a monthly data transfer limit (most of them do) then, if you get too many downloads, you could end up paying hefty charges for exceeding the monthly limit. To avoid this, don't export your MP3s at the highest possible sound quality. This keeps the file sizes as small as possible. You should also use your hosting firm's control panel to keep an eye on your site statistics so that you can see whether you're getting dangerously close to the limit. If you are, you could temporarily remove the download until things calm down again.

The principles of podcasting also apply to video blogging, although for video you'd use a video camera rather than an audio program. Video files are even bigger than sound files, though, so if you don't have a hosting deal with lots of data transfer each month then you might want to steer clear. It doesn't take many video downloads to break even the biggest data transfer limits.

Trackbacks

At the beginning of this section, we mentioned that some blogs list the other weblogs that link to them using a technique called a "trackback". Blogger doesn't offer either feature, although it's possible to add trackbacks if you install the Haloscan comments system. But what exactly are trackbacks?

Trackbacks are a way of telling a blogger that you've linked to one of their articles. Your blog sends their blog software a short message called a "ping", which says "Hi, I've just linked to you! You'll find my link here!". Once the ping has been received, your link will then appear in the list of trackbacks for that particular article.

There are two ways to use trackbacks: the hard way and the easy way. The hard way is in Blogger and requires installation of the Haloscan comments system from **www.haloscan.com**. When it's installed, the process goes something like this:

● Find a blog entry you want to send a trackback to.
● Look on the page for the trackback link.
● Copy the trackback ping address.
● Login to Haloscan and choose Manage Trackback.
● Click Send a Trackback Ping.
● Paste the Trackback URL into the appropriate field.
● Click Ping Now.

It's not exactly simple, is it?

Compare the above process with the way the Movable Type blogging system (**www.movabletype.org/siteuk**) can work if you've enabled Auto-Discovery in the blog preference:

● Write your blog post and include the link to the post you want to send a trackback to.
● Publish your post.

Movable Type automatically scans your post for links, and checks those links to see if it can find trackback ping addresses. If it finds them, it sends the necessary pings automatically. There is a way to do this with Haloscan, but it's not an official part of the service and requires a bit of fiddling with your Blogger template code.

Categories

Trackbacks aren't the only trick up Movable Type's sleeve. Movable Type makes it easy to assign categories to your blog entries and for your readers to browse those categories. It can publish site feeds in various versions of the RSS standard (Blogger only publishes in Atom format) and it can include files of any type in those feeds, which makes it ideal for publishing podcasts and video blogs. You can import old blog posts from Blogger and other blogging systems, create your blog in various different formats, and you can expand the program further with a range of plug-ins that add new features.

There are two downsides to Movable Type: it costs money (from £39.99), and you'll need to install it on your own web space. If you'd rather not do that, there's the TypePad service (**www.typepad.com/siteuk**), which combines Movable Type and web space and starts at £2.59 per month for the simplest version. If you want all the features, the Pro version is £7.59 per month.

Movable Type isn't the only option, though. If you feel you've outgrown Blogger but don't want to spend any money, WordPress (**www.wordpress.org**) offers similar power to Movable Type but is free of charge – although again you'll need your own web space to use it. It's a very powerful system that produces fantastic-looking weblogs, which explains why it's becoming very popular among prolific bloggers.

Movable Type and WordPress are both excellent blogging systems, and the choice between them is largely one of personal preference. However, for your first steps into blogging we'd still recommend using Blogger first: as both Movable Type and WordPress can import from Blogger, you'll be able to take your old blog entries with you if you decide to upgrade at a later date.

The free WordPress blogging system produces drop-dead gorgeous results and it's packed with powerful features for demanding bloggers.

Movable Type's excellent blogging system gives you complete control over everything you could possibly imagine.

5

PART 5

Writing your own web pages

The ABC of HTML

In this section we're going to tackle how to write the code for a web page by hand. The idea of writing code might seem a little daunting at first, like learning a secret language spoken only by geeks. However, creating a web page from scratch is not as complicated as it may seem, and it helps enormously to understand what's going on behind the scenes when your web design skills improve and you want to move beyond the confines of a WYSIWYG editor (see p.24). To create a web page, all you need is a web browser and a basic text editor such as Windows Notepad (which comes with every version of Windows) or TextEdit on a Mac.

Simple coding

Most web pages are written using a language called HTML, which stands for HyperText Markup Language. It's simpler than it sounds:

- The word "hypertext" refers to the fact that you can move around between pages on the web using *links*. Links are the words and images you can click on to get taken from one page to another or to jump around within a page. This ability to move around the web using these links is what makes it "hyper" text as opposed to regular text
- "Markup language" refers to the code, or markup, which you add to plain text on your web page in order to control how it is displayed and structured.

Coding a web page is similar to the process of adding formatting to a word-processing document. For example, consider a document in Microsoft Word. Here we can see several styles of text in the drop down menu.

The difference when creating a web page is that rather than adding styles using menus in a word processor, you add things called "tags" into the text itself. These tags are then read by the viewer's web browser, at which point the browser knows how to display the document onscreen. In other words, a web page's overall appearance is determined by the user's software, which makes it all the more critical that the web designer and the browser speak the same language. If there are mistakes or omissions in the markup, strange things happen.

Marking up a document is akin to adding styles to a document, as you might do in Microsoft Word.

Let's dive in for just a moment. Here we can see an example of a very basic web page in Windows Notepad. Don't worry if it looks complicated at first, as all will become clear very quickly:

You can write a web page in something as basic as Windows Notepad.

```
test.html - Notepad
File   Edit   Format   View   Help

<html>
<head><title>My First Web Page</title></head>
<body>

 <h1>Main Heading for the Page</h1>
 <p>First paragraph contains some text describing that this is my first web page.
    Even if this page seems very simple, soon I will be creating much more complex pages.</p>

 <h2>Here is a subheading</h2>
 <p>Here is a second paragraph under a subheading</p>

</body>
</html>
```

To start with, just focus on the bits from the fifth line down. The main heading is written between tags which say <h1> and </h1>. These tags indicate that anything in between them should be a level 1 heading. The subheading is inside tags that say <h2> and </h2>, indicating that anything between them should be a level 2 heading. And the paragraphs are inside tags that say <p> and </p>, thus marking the start and end of the paragraph. Note that an opening tag contains a coded instruction and a closing tag mimics it but includes a forward slash. This slash tells the browser to stop applying the tag's instructions at that point. Every opening tag must – well, certainly should – have a corresponding closing tag.

Here we can see what this page looks like in Internet Explorer.

So, when creating a web page you add tags to control the appearance of the page much as you would apply formatting to a Word document. However, rather than focusing on *styling* the document, which is what you do when formatting a word processed document, you need to think about the *structure* of the page.

A web page should describe its structure

While the example of a web page which you just saw was very basic, it does illustrate an important point: the markup in a web page should describe the structure of that page.

If you think about books for a moment, they tend to follow a structure that is loosely based around these lines:

A title that refers to the whole book
>A table of contents
>One or more chapters
>>Each chapter has its own title or heading
>>Under each chapter heading are often several sub headings
>>Inside the sub headings are paragraphs, images, possibly some lists of bullet points, and so on
>An index

The primary purpose of markup language is to describe the structure of a document in order that any web browser can display it correctly.

A brief history of HTML

Let's now backtrack briefly. When the web first came out it was quite a grey, dull place. There was little colour and images were rare. Its main purpose was to facilitate the easy exchange and retrieval of academic work to help researchers find information that might help them with their work and save them replicating studies unnecessarily.

However, as the web grew, all manner of people began to see personal and commercial potential for it. They started creating their own web pages to build online communities and to advertise companies and products. People wanted to be able to control the way that their web pages looked when viewed on a browser, and quite naturally they expected the same level of control as designers who create print publications. A web page should look just the same on computer A and computer B, quite regardless of whether one is a PC and the other is a Mac and one is running a particular web browser, like Microsoft Internet Explorer, and the other something quite different, like Netscape Navigator (as was).

As the desire and eventually the need to develop web pages increased, HTML expanded to not only describe the structure of documents but also to control their presentation: how pages looked, the colours used, the size of fonts, and so on.

All these new markup possibilities made web pages far more attractive. However, it also meant that web pages were designed to work only with desktop computers on which screens were roughly the same size. As the internet has evolved, people no longer just want to access the web via their desktop computers. They also want to be able to get information on their mobile phones, TV set-top boxes, handheld organisers, and all manner of other devices. The problem is that a web page controlled solely by HTML can look fantastic on a desktop monitor but be completely useless on a smaller screen.

As a consequence, web page authors are now strongly encouraged not to use markup language to control how their documents look. Rather, markup should describe the structure of a document, such as what is a heading and what is a paragraph. This doesn't mean that web pages have to be boring. Quite the contrary, in fact: we now have a better tool to style our web pages, the language of cascading style sheets, which we'll meet later in this book.

Cascading style sheets (or CSS) have several advantages over HTML, notably that you can create different style rules for different types of devices. This ensures that the same page can be displayed properly on just about anything from a widescreen plasma display to a mobile phone. We will see other advantages of CSS when we meet it later.

The same web page on a desktop PC and a mobile phone.

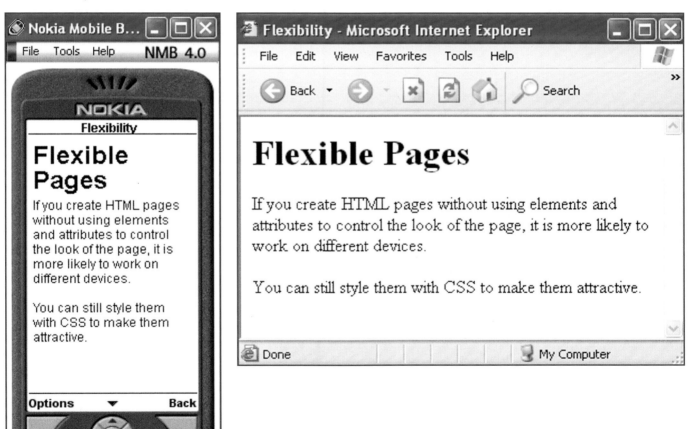

The difference between tags, elements and attributes

One thing that really helps with writing web pages is understanding the difference between tags, elements and attributes. Consider the following diagram:

Most elements are made up of an opening tag, a closing tag, and the content between the two tags.

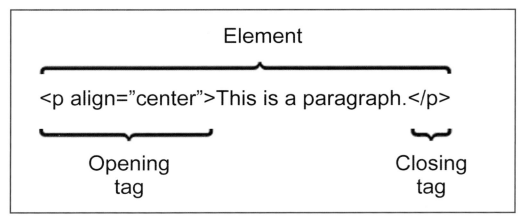

- The text in the paragraph is contained by two **tags:** an opening \<p\> tag and a closing \</p\> tag.
- The **element** is made up of the opening \<p\> and closing \</p\> *including the text between them*.
- The **attribute** sits inside the opening tag. In this case, it is an alignment attribute.

So just to be clear, a tag is a pair of angled brackets with letters written between these brackets e.g. \<p\>. Tags come in pairs: an opening tag and a closing tag. The closing tag differs from the opening tag because it has a forward slash character after the left angled bracket. Elements are opening and closing tags plus whatever is between them. Attributes are additional instructions contained within the opening tag in an element.

The attribute in our example indicates that the text in the paragraph should be aligned to the centre of the document, just like centring text in a word processor. (Note that the American English spelling of center is used in HTML.)

Attributes tend to follow a simple structure. They have:

- **An attribute name**. This is the property of the element that the attribute applies to, such as the alignment of text.
- **An attribute value**. This is the setting for this property, which for the align attribute can be left, right, center or justify.

There is always an equals sign separating the attribute name from its value and the value should be written within double quotes (although not all web page authors do this).

You will often see elements and attributes written in upper case, lower case, or indeed a mix of both. However, in XHTML (which we think of as being the most recent version of HTML), all element and attribute names should be written in lower case.

The skeleton of a web page

There are a few elements which you should always include whenever you create a web page. When we saw the first very basic example of a web page on p.113, we just looked at about half of the lines (the headings and the paragraphs). Let's go back to that example now, this time taking a look at the elements in the code.

Here is the code for that document again. The bits highlighted in grey are the parts that should appear in each document. We have indented elements that are inside other elements because it makes them easier to read.

```
<html>
 <head><title>My First Web Page</title></head>
 <body>

   <h1>Main Heading for the Page</h1>
   <p>First paragraph contains some text
      describing that this is my first web page.
      Even if this page seems very simple, soon I
      will be creating much more complex pages.</p>

   <h2>Here is a subheading</h2>
   <p>Here is a second paragraph under a
      subheading</p>

 </body>
</html>
```

So ... every HTML page should start with an opening <html> tag and end with a closing </html> tag. The page is contained within these two tags and is divided into two sections:

- The **head** of the document, contained between an opening <head> and a closing </head> tag. The head of the document contains information about the document but it is not actually visible when the page is viewed in a browser.
- The **body** of a document, contained between an opening <body> and closing </body> element. This is what you see in the browser window. In other words, it's the real content of the page.

Inside the <head> element there should be a <title> element. This is the page title and is usually displayed in the very top line of the browser window, outside the page content.

The <title> element is shown above the main browser menu.

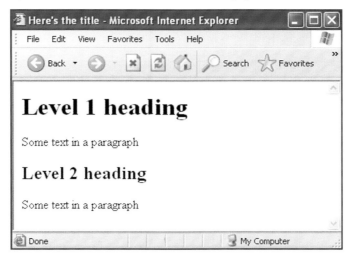

PART 5 Creating your first web page

Now that we know the basic structure of a web page,
let's try building one from scratch.

 1

Open up a text editor such as Windows Notepad (click Start >
Programs > Accessories > Notepad) or SimpleText or TextEdit
on a Mac.

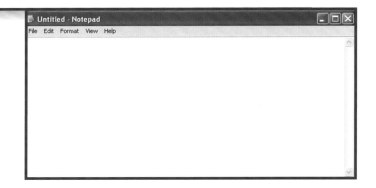

2

Enter the opening <html> tag at the top of the document, and
a closing </html> tag at the bottom, leaving a couple of blank
lines in between.

3

Add the opening and closing <head></head> tags followed by
the <body></body> tags. Indenting tags as shown here can
help you keep track of your code.

4

Inside the <head> element add the <title> element, with the words "My First Web Page" inside that. This completes the skeleton of the web page.

```
Untitled - Notepad
File  Edit  Format  View  Help
<html>
 <head><title>My First Web Page</title></head>

 <body></body>
</html>
```

5

Now we'll look at the main part of the page. Inside the <body> element add a <h1> element containing the words "My Home Page'. Again, indent the element to make the code clear.

```
Untitled - Notepad
File  Edit  Format  View  Help
<html>
 <head><title>My First Web Page</title></head>

 <body>
  <h1>My Home Page</h1>
 </body>
</html>
```

6

Add a <p> element after the <h1> element to create a paragraph. This paragraph should contain the words "Welcome to my first web page".

```
Untitled - Notepad
File  Edit  Format  View  Help
<html>
 <head><title>My First Web Page</title></head>

 <body>
  <h1>My Home Page</h1>
  <p>Welcome to my first web page</p>
 </body>
</html>
```

7

Save the file on your desktop as example1.html. If your text editor decides to save it as example.html.txt instead – that is, with a .txt extension at the end of the file name – put the name of the file in double quotes. This time it should save as a web page. Now start up your favourite web browser and go to the File menu. Select Open and browse to the file you just saved. You should see something like this: a bona fide web page created with nothing but HTML code in a text editor. Congratulations!

PART 5 Taking it further

Having seen the basic structure of a web page and learned the difference between elements (which are made up of tags and what is between those tags) and attributes, you can quickly look at a whole range of other elements, and start creating far more complicated and interesting documents.

But before we press on, note that you can learn a lot about web page structure simply by looking at how other people go about writing their web pages. This is because browsers have an option which reveals the source code behind a page. In Internet Explorer go to the View menu, and select the View Source option. Here we can see the source code for the website homepage of the W3C (the body that controls the development of HTML).

Viewing the source of pages is a great way to learn more.

If you have already had a look at the source of some web pages, you might have seen the <body> element carry all kinds of attributes, such as bgcolor (which can be used to set the background colour of the document) or leftmargin (which is just one way to offset the page from the edge of the browser window). But remember that we are not using attributes to change the appearance of our documents. Rather, as we shall see, that is a job for CSS.

You might also see elements called <script>, which usually contain a language called JavaScript. Unfortunately, there is not space to go into scripting in this book.

Using elements to markup text

In this section, we will take a closer look at several elements that can be used to describe the structure of a web page. Keep focussing on that word *structure* as you read through this section: we are trying to describe the overall layout of the documents, not its appearance.

<h1> to <h6> contain headings

In the same way that your word processor has several "levels" of heading, starting with heading 1 for the primary heading, heading 2 for section headings, heading 3 for sub-headings within sections and so on, there are six levels of heading in HTML. These are represented using the elements <h1> to <h6>.

By default, a browser will display <h1> elements in the largest size and <h6> elements in the smallest, as you can see here:

How a browser renders heading elements.

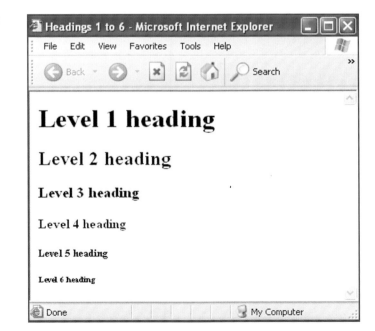

<p> contains paragraphs

As we have already seen, each heading is likely to be followed by one or more paragraphs of text. The opening <p> tag indicates the start of a paragraph, while the end of a paragraph is shown with a closing </p> tag.

**
 creates a line break**

The <br /> element creates a line break (a bit like pressing the return key when using a word processor). The <br /> element is a special kind of element because it does not need a closing tag. It is referred to as an "empty element". Empty elements need to be written with a space and a forward slash character before the right angled bracket.

You could write sentences on consecutive lines like so:

Line one
Line two
Line three
Line four
Line five

Sometimes you might see a line break simply written <br>, but it is good practice to write them correctly, like this: <br />.

Creating line breaks with the <br /> element.

<pre> creates preformatted text

One interesting thing about web browsers is that they will only show one space between two words, even if you type 20 spaces in your web page. However, if you want the spaces to be preserved in part of a page, then you can write that content in a <pre> element.

The real purpose of a <pre> element is to preserve the precise formatting of the text when this is important to its understanding, such as when writing computer code. It should not be used simply to add line breaks (for which you should use the <br /> element), or to indent text (for which you should use CSS).

As this screenshot shows, browsers tend to format the contents of a <pre> element in a type of font referred to as "monospace". In a monospace font, each letter is the same width whereas, in other fonts, letters like "m" are wider than letters like "l".

You can retain spaces and line breaks using a <pre> element.

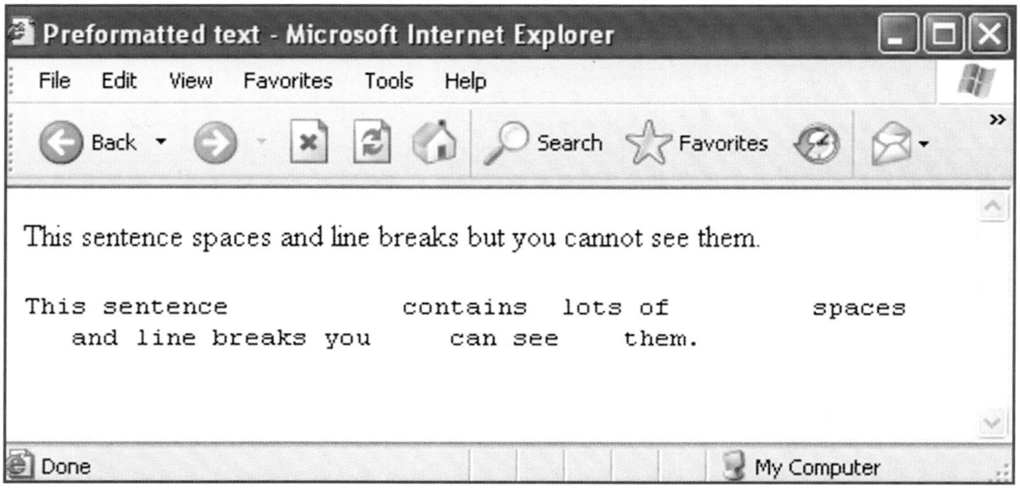

Presentational elements

Now let's take a look at some elements that affect the presentation of text. These are fairly self-explanatory, so they are just listed in the following table.

Element	Purpose
<b>	Bold. The content of the element will be displayed in a bold typeface.
<i>	Italic. The content of the element will be displayed in an italic typeface.
<u>	Underline. The content of the element will be underlined.
<strike>	Strikethrough. The content of the element will have a line through the centre of the font.
<sup>	Superscript. The content of the element will be shown in superscript (a smaller font that looks higher than the rest of the text on that line). It is commonly used with dates, as in 12th.
<sub>	Subscript. The content of the element will be shown in subscript (a smaller font which looks lower that the rest of the text on that line). It is commonly used to denote footnotes.
<small>	The content of the element will be shown smaller than the surrounding text.
<big>	The content of the element will be shown bigger than the surrounding text.
<hr />	An empty element that creates a horizontal line, also known as a horizontal rule.

Here is an example that makes use of some of the presentational elements:

```
<html>
    <head><title>Presentational
    Elements</title></head>
    <body>
        <b>Here is some bold text</b><br />
        <i>Here is some italic text</i><br />
        <u>This text is underlined</u><br />
        <strike>This text has a line through
        it</strike><br />
        You can add superscript text, for things
        such as dates: 12<sup>th</sup> July<br />
        You can add subscript for things like
        footnotes <sub>2</sub><br />
        You can make some text <small>smaller than
        the text</small> surrounding it<br />
        You can make some text <big>bigger than the
        text</big> surrounding it<br />
        <hr />
    </body>
</html>
```

You can see what this page looks like here:

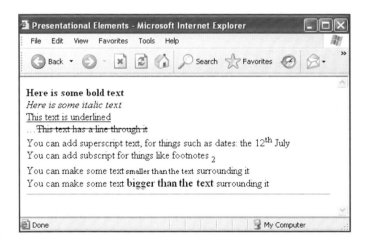

Presentational elements affect the look of their contents.

Phrase elements

Phrase elements add to the meaning of the document. Some of these elements will be displayed slightly differently in a web browser, although they should never be used for the way they make text look. Again, appearance is the role of CSS.

In fact, a couple of these elements are not for the benefit of those looking at websites, but rather for other types of program.

Element	Purpose
<em>	Emphasis. This indicates that the content of this element should have emphasis. Voice browsers (used by the blind) would add emphasis when reading the content of this element. Most browsers show emphasis in italic text.
<strong>	Strong emphasis. As with the <em> element, this adds emphasis, but this time it is strong emphasis. Most browsers show this in bold text.
<address>	Address. You should place addresses inside an address element to help automated applications (such as search engines) isolate addresses in web pages.
<code>	Computer code. This will tend to be preformatted and shown in a fixed-width font such as courier.

Here is an example that uses phrase elements:

```
<html>
    <head><title>Phrase Elements</title></head>
    <body>
        You can add <em>emphasis</em><br />
        You can add <strong>strong
        emphasis</strong><br /><br />
        The Queen of England's main residence is
        <address>Buckingham Palace, Buckingham
        Palace Road, London, SW1A 1AA,
        UK</address><br /><br />
        Code has a special element
        <code>print()</code>
    </body>
</html>
```

You can see what this example looks like in a browser in this screenshot:

Phrase elements add meaning to their content.

Lists

If you want to add a list to your web page, with either bullet points or numbers, then there are some special elements that allow you to do this.

Element	Purpose
<ul>	Unordered list, denoted with bullet points
<ol>	Ordered list, numbered
<li>	List item, delimiting each separate entry in the list

Here we have an example of ordered and unordered lists:

```
<html>
   <head><title>Example of lists</title></head>
   <body>

   Here is an example of a bulleted list:
   <ul>
      <li>Bullet point one</li>
      <li>Bullet point two</li>
      <li>Bullet point three</li>
   </ul>

   Here is an example of a numbered list:
   <ol>
      <li>Item number one</li>
      <li>Item number two</li>
      <li>Item number three</li>
   </ol>

   </body>
</html>
```

There are also a couple of handy attributes that you might like to be aware of when creating numbered lists. The type attribute sits in the opening <ol> tag and allows you to specify what numbers you want to use. For example:

Attribute	Purpose
<ol type="1">	Creates numbers (1, 2, 3)
<ol type="A">	Creates upper case letters (A, B, C)
<ol type="a">	Creates lower case letters (a, b, c)
<ol type="I">	Creates upper case Roman numerals (I, II, III
<ol type="i">	Creates lower case Roman numerals (i, ii, iii)

You can also indicate what number you want your list to start at by using the start attribute. This sits in the opening <ol> tag in an ordered list. For example, the following list would start with the number 3:

```
<ol start="3">
   <li>list item 3</li>
   <li>list item 4</li>
   <li>list item 5</li>
</ol>
```

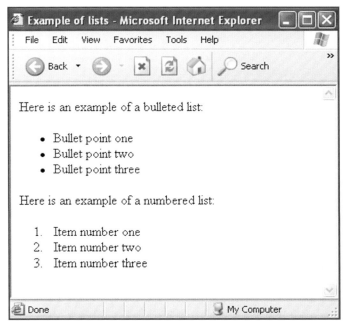

You can create bullet points and numbered lists.

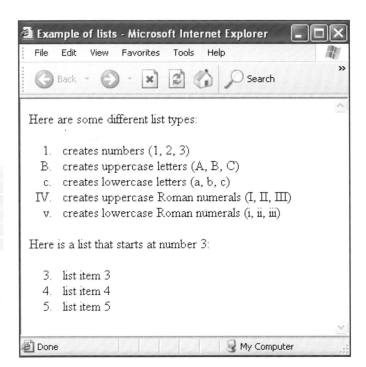

You can select the type of numbered list and the starting number.

The <font> element

As we mentioned earlier in the chapter, some elements were introduced into HTML just to grant web page authors the ability to control the presentation of their pages. One such element was the <font> element which allows you to specify what kind of typeface you want to use in your document (for example, to specify that text should be shown in Arial, Courier or some other typeface). While it is now generally considered better to use CSS rather than HTML to control the presentation of your pages, you will still often see the <font> element used.

The <font> element can carry several useful attributes, such as:

- **Face**. This value is a comma-separated list of typefaces, starting with your first choice and then stating alternatives. A browser can only display any given typeface if that font is installed on the computer, so it pays to give alternatives and to stick to commonly used fonts rather than going for something exotic.
- **Size**. This value determines the size of the typeface, ranging from 1 (smallest) to 6 (largest).
- **Color**. This value controls the typeface colour. Note the American spelling.

For example, you might see a page that uses the <font> element like so:

```
<html>
   <head><title>A page that uses the font
   element</title></head>
   <body>
      <font face="arial, verdana, sans-serif"
      size="6" color="red">Heading goes
      here</font><br>
      <font face="times, times new roman, serif"
      size="2" color="black">The text underneath
      the heading goes here.</font>
   </body>
</html>
```

You can see what this page would look like here:

The <font> element is still widely used, but you should try to use CSS, rather than markup, to control the presentation of pages.

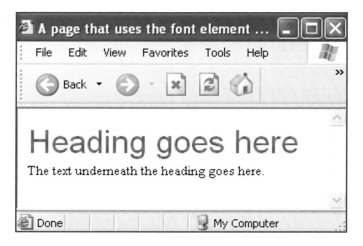

Creating links between pages

One of the most powerful features of the web has long been and remains hyperlinks (or just links, for short), by which we mean text or images that you can click on to move to another page. Although we take links for granted, without the ability to link between documents the web would not have been anywhere near as popular as it is today.

In this section we will be looking at how to create four types of links:

● Links from your page to another website
● Links to other pages on your own site
● Links to a specific part of a page
● Email links

Creating links to other websites

If you want to add a link to another website, you can do this with the <a>, the anchor, element. When people click on the text between the opening <a> tag and the closing </a> tag they get transported to another page.

The address of the page you want to link to is specified using the href attribute. For example, the following would create a link to the Google website:

```
<a href="http://www.google.com">Google is a
popular search engine</a>
```

The text between the <a> tags becomes a clickable link.

As we can see from the screenshot, by default the text between the opening <a> tag and the closing </a> tag is usually shown in blue in the browser, and will be underlined. We will learn later how to change the presentation of links using CSS.

You can change the behaviour of a hyperlink so that clicking it opens the new web page in a new browser window (rather than replacing the current page with the new page). To do this, use the target attribute and give it a value of _blank, like so:

```
<a href="http://www.google.com"
target="_blank">Google is a popular search
engine</a>
```

This link will look exactly the same as the previous one when viewed on the page, but it will open in a new browser window. You should avoid opening too many pages in new windows as web users can get very confused if there are lots of windows open at the same time. As a result, most web page authors avoid opening new windows for web pages on their own site, and only create a new window if they are linking to another site altogether.

Creating links to pages on your own site

Creating links to pages on your own site can be even easier than creating links to other sites. If you have several web pages that are all in the same folder, you only need to put the name of the file in the value of the href attribute on the opening <a> tag. For example, here is a link to a page call ContactUs.html that lives in the same folder as this page:

```
<a href="ContactUs.html">Contact details</a>
```

However, if you have a large site with lots of pages, you are likely to want to arrange these pages into separate folders in order to help you keep track of each of the pages. For example, a music website might have the following sections: home page, news, reviews, events, contact us.

If the site owners regularly update its content, they might put the news, reviews and events each in their own separate folders to help keep track of the pages. The folder structure might look something like the one shown in this screenshot:

Large sites can separate their page sections, each with their own folder.

The home page in this case is called index.html. The home page is not in a folder, so in order to link to a news page called news.html in the news folder, the link should specify the name of the folder followed by a forward slash followed by the name of the file in that folder:

```
<a href="news/news.html">News Home Page</a>
```

And if this same news page wanted to link back to the main home page called index.html then that link would start with two dots and a forward slash, to indicate that the file was in the parent folder:

```
<a href="../index.html">News Home Page</a>
```

These partial addresses (which do not start with a domain name, such as **http://www.haynes.co.uk**) are known as **relative addresses** because they point to pages in **relation** to the position of this page. There are two great advantages to using relative URLs on your own site:

- They are much shorter and are therefore quicker to write.
- If your domain name changes (which can happen if you get a new hosting company) you do not have to rewrite all of your links. They will continue to work so long as you preserve your folder structure.

Creating links to parts of pages

You have probably seen some web pages that contain links to specific parts of the same page. For example, a long page might have a list of links at the top of the page to help you find the appropriate part of the page (FAQ pages are a good example of this).

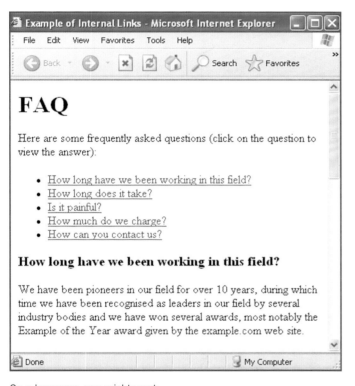

On a long page, you might want to create a link to a specific part of the page.

In such cases there are two parts to the links:

- **Source**: the link the user clicks on to get taken to another part of a page.
- **Destination**: the part of the page they will arrive at.

Both are created with the <a> element, but they carry different attributes. Let's have a look at the destination link first, because without that we don't have a specific part of the page to link to.

The destination part of the link is an <a> element in the part of the document you want to link to. When the <a> element is a destination, it should have two attributes: name and id. The value of these attributes should be the same and it should be a name/word to identify that part of the page. For example, on long pages you might create a destination at the top of your page, and create a link from the bottom of the page back up to the top. In this case, let's say you want to return a visitor to your first heading, like so:

```
<a name="top" id="top"><h1>My Home Page</h1></a>
```

The words "My Home Page" are thus marked up as a destination. With the destination in place, you can now add the source part of the link further down the page so that when people click the link, the browser window will scroll back up to "My Home Page" (the destination).

When source links are pointing to a part of the same page, they have an href attribute whose value starts with a # sign, like so:

```
<a href="#top">Back to top</a>
```

The viewer will now see the phrase "Back to top" as an underlined blue hyperlink on the page; and when they click it, they'll be whisked back to the top of the page.

You can also link to a specific part of *another* page in your website. For example, if you had a long FAQ page, you might want to link *to* a specific question on that part of the page *from* several places on the site. The question is thus the destination.

If one of the items in your FAQ was your contact details, the relevant part of the FAQ page (which is called faq.html) might look like this:

```
<a name="contact" id="contact"><h2>How to contact us</h2></a>
<p>You can call us on 0800 000 000 or email help@example.com</p>
```

This is the destination, marked up with a name and id attributes. You could then link to this part of the faq.html page using a source link like this:

```
<a href="faq.html#contact">How to contact us</a>
```

Note the syntax. The file name (i.e. the name of the web page we want to link to) is followed by the # symbol followed by the value of the name or id attribute on the destination.

Creating links to send emails

You can even create special links that launch the visitor's default email program. To create an email link you need to use the `<a>` element again. Users can click on whatever is written between the opening `<a>` tag and the closing `</a>` tag in order to send the email.

This time, the value of the href attribute starts with the keyword mailto, followed by a colon, followed by the email address you are sending the message to:

```
<a href="mailto:info@example.com">Send me an
email</a>
```

All you would see in the browser is a link that says send me an email. When the user clicks it, their email program will open a new, blank email addressed to the specified email address.

You can even create links that add a pre-determined subject line to the email. In order to do this, add a question mark after the email address, followed by the subject of the message. Note that if your subject line contains spaces, as it will if it's more than one word, you must replace the spaces with the characters %20, like so:

```
<a href="mailto:info@example.com?subject=website
%20enquiry">Send me an email</a>
```

You can use email links to encourage users to send you emails.

PART **5**

Adding images to your pages

Images really help liven up any website. If pages are too text heavy, they can put visitors off. Photos, logos and images for the main navigation all have a place and images can be made into clickable links in much the same way as text.

However, you should be careful about your use of images. If you use too many, or if they are too large, the page will be slow to load. This is less of a problem if your visitors are coming to your site over a broadband internet connection but this should not be taken for granted.

The <img /> element

You can insert images into your pages using the <img /> element. It is another example of an empty element (like the <br /> and <hr /> elements) and therefore only one tag is used. This tag should carry several attributes, and it should end with a space and a forward slash before the right angled bracket.

Images should generally be stored along with the pages of your site, and they are often put in a special folder called **images** (or sometimes called assets). Here we can see a folder structure for the music site we discussed on p.128, this time with an added images folder.

Images are often placed in a folder of their own. In this case, you can see an images folder.

The name of the image that you want to use is given as the value of an attribute called src. For example, if you want to add a logo (logo.gif) to the home page of the music site (index.html), and that image was in the images folder, you could do it like so:

```
<img src="images/logo.gif" />
```

You can see that the image is identified in the same way as the relative URLs we met on p.128-9. If you wanted to add this same image to a page in the news folder called news.html, then you would write it like so:

```
<img src="../images/logo.gif" />
```

In this case, the ../ indicates that we need to go up a folder and then look in the images folder.

<img /> elements should also always carry an alt attribute. The value of the alt attribute is a text description for the image, so this element might look like this:

```
<img src="../images/logo.gif" alt="MyMusicSite
Logo" />
```

Ideally, you should also control the width and the height of the image here, measured in pixels. These measurements are given in width and height attributes, like so:

```
<img src="../images/logo.gif" alt="MyMusicSite
Logo" width="150" height="40" />
```

This shows an image that is 150 pixels wide and 40 pixels high. To find the size of an existing image, simply open it in your web browser, right click it and select Properties. Here you will see an option that says Dimensions.

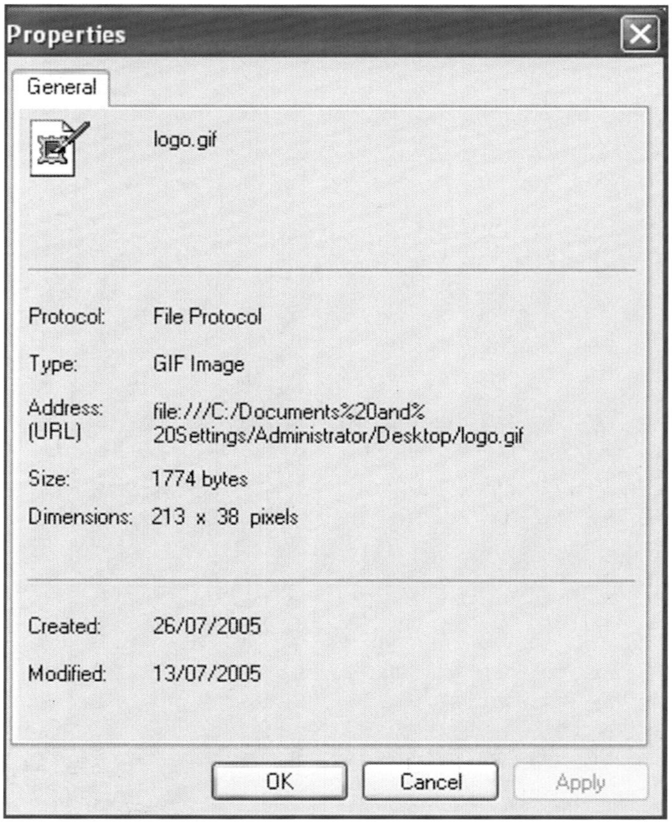

Right-clicking an image in a browser and selecting the Properties option shows you the image dimensions. You can change these with the width and height attributes.

Properties

General

logo.gif

Protocol:	File Protocol
Type:	GIF Image
Address: (URL)	file:///C:/Documents%20and%20Settings/Administrator/Desktop/logo.gif
Size:	1774 bytes
Dimensions:	213 x 38 pixels
Created:	26/07/2005
Modified:	13/07/2005

OK   Cancel   Apply

What types of image to use

There are lots of image formats that you can choose from, but it is best to stick to two types of image for the web: GIF and JPEG. As a rule of thumb, use GIF images for graphics that contain a lot of flat colour (for example, a logo with areas that have the same shade of red) and JPEGs for photographs. This is because GIF images will save to smaller file sizes when parts of the photo use exactly the same colours, and JPEGs are better for saving images where there are lots of different colours.

Many browsers also support a format called PNG, which was designed to be the successor to the GIF image. Unfortunately, image formats other than GIF and JPEG work in some browsers but not in others, and so are best avoided. Any good image manipulation program (such as Photoshop or Paint Shop Pro) will allow you to save images as GIFs or JPEGs.

It is worth noting that the maximum computer screen resolution is 72 dots per inch (72dpi), which is a lot lower than print resolution. Images with a higher resolution than 72dpi will take longer to load than necessary and will not look any better on screen. Use your image editor to reduce the resolution to 72dpi before using images on the web.

If your image is a photo you should use a JPEG.

If an image contains sections that are exactly the same colour, you should save it as a GIF. This is typically used for computer-generated graphics.

Using images as links

You can put an image between an opening <a> tag and a closing </a> tag to make an image a link. If you do, you should also add a border attribute with a value of 0 otherwise you will find a blue line drawn around the edge of your image. For example:

```
<a href="index.html"><img
src="../images/logo.gif" alt="MyMusicSite Logo"
border="0" /></a>
```

This screenshot shows you an example of two images, the first without a border attribute, and the second with a border attribute whose value is 0.

If you make an image a link, you will have to add a border attribute to prevent an unsightly blue line appearing around the edge of it.

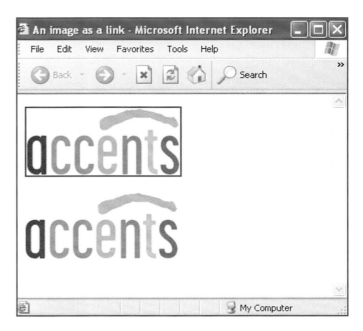

Where to get images

It can be very hard to find strong images that really set off your site. However, it is well worth spending the time on getting the right images as it can make the difference between an average site and a great site.

Generally speaking you cannot just copy images from other people's sites. This would be breaking copyright law. Many professional web designers either pay for the right to use photos from what is known as a stock photography library (such as **www.gettyimages.com** or **www.corbis.com**) or sometimes even commission original photographs.

However, there are some good resources on the web where you can find very cheap images. iStockPhoto, **www.iStockPhoto.com**, was set up for web designers to get cheap stock photography and for photographers and illustrators to sell their pictures. Prices start at US$1 per photo (compared to the £50+ per photo charged by many image libraries). See also p.41.

www.iStockPhoto.com is a great resource for finding good quality, reasonably priced images for your sites.

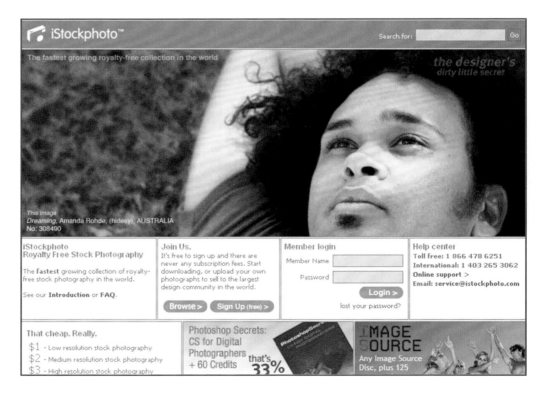

PART 5

Adding tables to your pages

The ability to create tables is a very handy part of a web designer's toolkit. There are two main reasons why you might want to add tables to your site:

● You have some tabular data, which is best organised in rows and columns, such as sporting results or research findings.
● You want to control the layout of your pages, in which case tables can be used to position items on your page.

We're going to take a look at creating tables for tabular data first.

Tables for tabular data

Tables are created using an element called – no surprises here – <table>. The table is held between the opening <table> tag and a closing </table> tag. Between these tags, tables are written out one row at a time, using the <tr> element to create a table row. Each row is then made up of individual table cells, from left to right. These cells are created using one of two elements:

● The <th> element indicates a table heading
● The <td> element indicates a table data cell

As with the other elements we met earlier, the content must go between the opening and closing tags. Take a look at this simple table:

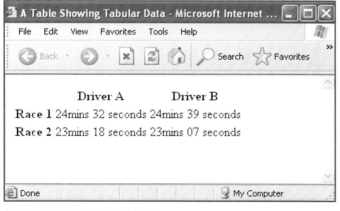

A table with three rows and three columns.

Here is the code used to create this page. Note how the markup for the tables is indented, as this makes it easier to read:

```
<table>
    <tr>
        <td></td>
        <th>Driver A</th>
        <th>Driver B</th>
    </tr>
    <tr>
        <th>Race 1</th>
        <td>24 mins 32 seconds</td>
        <td>24 mins 39 seconds </td>
    </tr>
    <tr>
        <th>Race 2</th>
        <td>23 mins 18 seconds </td>
        <td>23 mins 07 seconds </td>
    </tr>
</table>
```

As you can see the entire table is contained within a <table> element. The three rows each start with an opening <tr> tag and end with a closing </tr> tag. Inside each row are three more elements. Some of these are headings, others are table data.

Each row should have the same number of cells, even if some of those cells are empty (whether they are <th> or <td> elements).

Table borders and spacing

The table element can carry a border attribute to determine the width of the border in pixels. For example, to create a table with no border you would have the following:

```
<table border="0">
```

To have a 10 pixel wide border you would have the following:

```
<table border="10">
```

You can add space between each of the cells using the cellspacing attribute. The value of this attribute is the gap between cells in pixels:

```
<table border="2" cellspacing="10">
```

You can add space between the edge of the cell and what is written inside it using the cellpadding attribute:

```
<table border="2" cellpadding="10">
```

Here you can see some examples of different borders, cellpaddings, and cellspacings:

You can easily control the appearance of your tables.

Table and cell widths

You can control the width of the entire table with the width attribute on the <table> element, and you can control the width of columns by using the width attribute on the first set of <td> or <th> elements in the table (note that you cannot have different widths for cells in different rows).

```
<table width="500" border="1">
   <tr>
      <td width="250"></td>
      <th width="125">Driver A</th>
      <th width="125">Driver B</th>
   </tr>
   <tr>
      <th>Race 1</th>
      <td>24 mins 32 seconds</td>
      <td>24 mins 39 seconds </td>
   </tr>
   <tr>
      <th>Race 2</th>
      <td>23 mins 18 seconds </td>
      <td>23 mins 07 seconds </td>
   </tr>
</table>
```

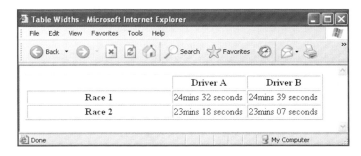

Controlling the width of tables and cells.

Using tables for layout

As you can see, tables create a grid. Often when print designers are creating a page layout they will use a **layout grid**, which divides pages into columns and rows. For example, traditional newspapers often display articles in columns. Web designers do something very similar by using tables to layout web pages. It helps them to create columns of text and images that sit next to each other.

Here you can see an example of a site designed with borderless (and thus invisible) tables:

Research has showed that people have difficulty reading large amounts of text on the web, especially when they are shown in wide lines, so restricting the width of text makes it easier on the eye. It can also make the page look more attractive. Here is the same page designed without a table in place to control the positioning of the text.

Using a table is also one way of ensuring that your page remains a fixed width; no matter what the size of the viewer's browser window, you can control the way your page content is displayed by placing it within a fixed-width table.

You can control the layout of your pages with tables.

Same page as before – but this time without using tables.

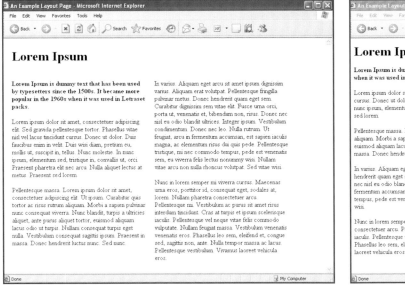

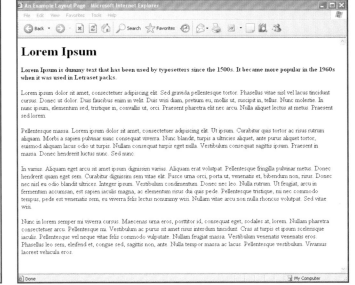

Vertical alignment of text

If the cells on a row contain different amounts of text, vertical text positioning defaults to the middle of the cell. You can make text align from the top of the cell, which generally looks better, using the valign attribute (this attribute can also take values of middle and bottom).

Nesting elements

As we have seen, most elements, with the exception of empty elements such as <br /> and <hr />, have starting and ending tags. It is very important to write these tags symmetrically – or to give it the correct term, to make sure that they nest correctly.

If you place an element within another element, both the opening and closing tags must appear within that element. So if you want some bold text in a paragraph, for example, your opening and closing <b> tags both need to be inside the <p> element.

An example would probably help here. The following is correct, because both the opening and closing tag of the <b> element are inside the <p> element:

```
<p>At the end of this paragraph is some <b>bold
text</b></p>
```

However, the following is incorrect, because the closing <b> tag is outside the closing <p> tag:

```
<p>At the end of this paragraph is some <b>bold
text</p></b>
```

While most browsers would still display this example as you would hope, it is technically incorrect, and it is a good idea to get into the habit of closing all elements correctly.

PART 5

Creating your first site – using HTML

In this workshop, we are going to put together what we have learned so far and create a very simple two-page site. The first page will introduce the subject – you – and the second page will talk about your hobbies and interests:

①

Open up your text editor (such as Windows Notepad or TextEdit). We will start by creating a home page that introduces you.

Untitled - Notepad
File Edit Format View Help

②

Add the skeleton of the page, the <html>, <head>, <title> and <body> elements. The title of the page will be your name followed by the words "Home Page".

Untitled - Notepad
File Edit Format View Help

```
<html>
  <head><title>Tom Smith's Home Page</title></head>
  <body>


  </body>
</html>
```

③

In the body of the page, we will put an <h1> element to contain the title of the page. This will be followed by a <p> element containing the name of this page and a link to the second page of the site. This content of this paragraph is what allows users to understand the structure of the site and navigate it. You can see from a glance that there is a Home page (this page) and a page about your hobbies. To get the hobby page, simply click on this link. You could easily add more pages to the site by adding more links to this section when you have created the page.

Untitled - Notepad
File Edit Format View Help

```
<html>
  <head><title>Tom Smith's Home Page</title></head>
  <body>

  <h1>Tom Smith's Home Page</h1>
  <p>Home Page | <a href="hobbies.html">My hobbies</a></p>

  </body>
</html>
```

4

Next add in an introductory paragraph introducing yourself, your name and age, where you live, and where you work.

```
Untitled - Notepad
File  Edit  Format  View  Help
<html>
 <head><title>Tom Smith's Home Page</title></head>
 <body>

 <h1>Tom Smith's Home Page</h1>
 <p>Home Page | <a href="hobbies.html">My hobbies</a></p>

 <p>My name is Tom Smith, I am 52, and I live in Birmingham in the middle of the UK. I am
a the head chef of The Bistro in the four star Watts Hotel in the centre of town.|</p>

 </body>
</html>
```

5

Add a paragraph about your family. Inside this paragraph, add an <img /> element linking to a picture of yourself. Make sure that the photo is stored in the same folder on your computer as this page. Speaking of which...

```
Untitled - Notepad
File  Edit  Format  View  Help
<html>
 <head><title>Tom Smith's Home Page</title></head>
 <body>

 <h1>Tom Smith's Home Page</h1>
 <p>Home Page | <a href="hobbies.html">My hobbies</a></p>

 <p>My name is Tom Smith, I am 52, and I live in Birmingham in the middle of the UK. I am
a the head chef of The Bistro in the four star Watts Hotel in the centre of town. </p>

 <p><img src="tom.jpg" width="100" height="133" alt="photo of me" />I have been married
to Jane for 27 years, and we have two lovely children: Martin aged 14, and Alice aged 12.
Jane and I met when I was training to be a chef, she used to work for a local grocers.</p>

 </body>
</html>
```

6

Save this page as index.html. As just mentioned, this file and the photo should be saved in the same folder.

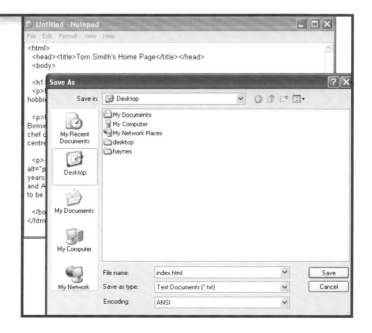

7

Now open a second blank page in your text editor and add in the skeleton of the HTML document. This time the title of the page should be your name followed by the word "Hobbies".

```
Untitled - Notepad
File  Edit  Format  View  Help

<html>
  <head><title>Tom Smith's Hobbies</title></head>
  <body>


  </body>
</html>
```

8

Again, add a level 1 heading, followed by a paragraph containing the names of the pages in the site. This time, the "Home Page" text should have an <a> element to make a link to the home page.

```
Untitled - Notepad
File  Edit  Format  View  Help

<html>
  <head><title>Tom Smith's Hobbies</title></head>
  <body>

  <h1>Tom Smith's Hobbies</h1>
  <p><a href="index.html">Home Page | My hobbies</p>

  </body>
</html>
```

9

Add an unordered list, with at least three points. Each of these points should contain the name of one of your hobbies.

```
Untitled - Notepad
File  Edit  Format  View  Help

<html>
  <head><title>Tom Smith's Hobbies</title></head>
  <body>

  <h1>Tom Smith's Hobbies</h1>
  <p><a href="index.html">Home Page | My hobbies</p>

  <ul>
    <li>Cooking</li>
    <li>Football</li>
    <li>The internet</li>
  </ul>

  </body>
</html>
```

10

For each of these points, add a level 2 heading, followed by a paragraph about that hobby.

```
Untitled - Notepad
File  Edit  Format  View  Help

  <h2>Cooking</h2>
  <p>I have been a working chef for over 25 years, and to be a good chef you simply have to
  love food. From finding the best ingredients, through preparing a meal, to eating the meal, I
  am passionate about every aspect of food and cooking. My favourite food is fresh Dover
  sole.</p>

  <h2>Football</h2>
  <p>I have supported Arsenal ever since growing up in Highbury in North London. My family
  have been Gunners fans for as long as we know. As a child I used to go to every home
  match with my grandfather, a live-long season ticket holder. When we could we would also
  go to away matches. Living up in Birmingham, I no longer get the chance to see as many
  matches, but I still watch as many as I can on TV.</p>

  <h2>The internet</h2>
  <p>Ever since we got a computer for the kids to do their school work on, they have been
  trying to keep me off it. I love finding new recipes, and keeping up with football on the web,
  and I do lots of shopping online too, I even booked our family holiday online.</p>
```

Around each <h2> element add a destination anchor, so that you can link directly to this part of the page.

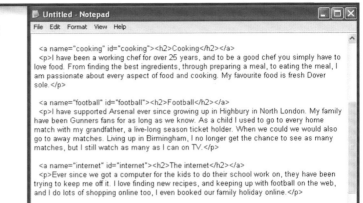

```
<a name="cooking" id="cooking"><h2>Cooking</h2></a>
<p>I have been a working chef for over 25 years, and to be a good chef you simply have to
love food. From finding the best ingredients, through preparing a meal, to eating the meal, I
am passionate about every aspect of food and cooking. My favourite food is fresh Dover
sole.</p>

<a name="football" id="football"><h2>Football</h2></a>
<p>I have supported Arsenal ever since growing up in Highbury in North London. My family
have been Gunners fans for as long as we know. As a child I used to go to every home
match with my grandfather, a live-long season ticket holder. When we could we would also
go to away matches. Living up in Birmingham, I no longer get the chance to see as many
matches, but I still watch as many as I can on TV.</p>

<a name="internet" id="internet"><h2>The internet</h2></a>
<p>Ever since we got a computer for the kids to do their school work on, they have been
trying to keep me off it. I love finding new recipes, and keeping up with football on the web,
and I do lots of shopping online too, I even booked our family holiday online.</p>
```

In the <li> elements at the top of the page, add links to these destination anchors, so people can skip directly to each part of the page.

```
<html>
  <head><title>Tom Smith's Hobbies</title></head>
  <body>

  <h1>Tom Smith's Hobbies</h1>
  <p><a href="index.html">Home Page | My hobbies</p>

  <ul>
    <li><a href="#cooking">Cooking</a></li>
    <li><a href="#cooking">Football</a></li>
    <li><a href="#cooking">The internet</a></li>
  </ul>
```

Save the file as hobbies.html.

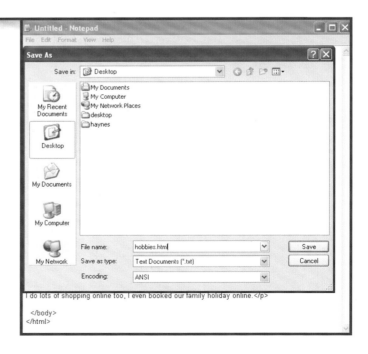

Open up index.html in your browser, and you can now see and browse your first small site. OK, it's not actually on the internet but traditional sites are usually designed and built offline like this (unlike blogs, which are created and developed live online). We'll return to this point later.

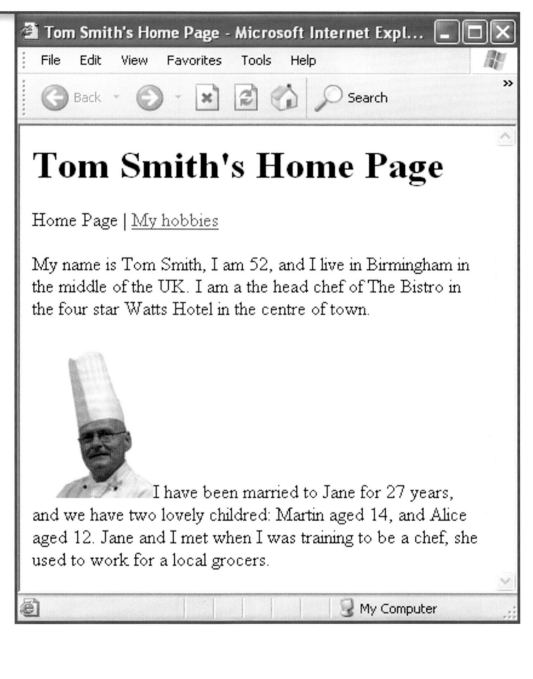

PART 6 # Adding style to your documents

PART 6 Style sheets

We've looked at how to markup text and create document structures, and how to create links and add images to web pages. It's about time we thought about making pages more attractive.

In order to control the presentation of the pages we need to work with a language that is used in conjunction with HTML. This is called CSS or Cascading Style Sheets.

A cascading style sheet is made up of rules that are applied to the content of certain elements in order to indicate how these elements should be formatted. For example, you might set rules that control the typeface used for the content of the <h1> element, making all level one headings a different style from the rest of the text on the page. Similarly, you might want to set the background colour of table heading elements so that they stand out from the rest of the table.

These rules can be placed inside the <head> element of a document using an element called <style>. However, you are generally better off creating a separate CSS file which can then be linked to and referenced by all your HTML pages. This is the approach we will be taking. All we need, again, is a text editor like Notepad.

How to link to a style sheet

You can use the same CSS style sheet with all the pages on your site. This can save a great deal of work because you do not have to put markup in each separate page to indicate how the page should look. To link to a CSS file from your HTML documents, you need to put a <link /> element inside the <head> element on each page. The <link /> element is an empty element:

```
<link rel="stylesheet" type="text/css"
href="styles.css" />
```

The <link /> element is not only used with style sheets, so it carries three attributes that describe the document being linked to:

- The rel attribute (short for relationship). This indicates the relationship between the current document and the one in the link. In this case, it indicates that the document being linked to is a style sheet for this document.
- The type attribute. This indicates the media type of document that is being linked to. In this case the file is a style sheet, which is a text document (as opposed to a JPEG, an MP3 or some other kind of file).
- The href attribute. This determines where the style sheet can be found. Here the style sheet is called "styles.css" and is in the same folder as the page.

Advantages of using external style sheets

Here are just a few of the advantages you achieve by using external style sheets to control the presentation of your web pages rather than using markup in your HTML documents that controls presentation of pages:

- You can use the same style sheet with several HTML pages rather than repeating the rules in each page.
- You can easily update the look of a whole site simply by updating the rules in the style sheet (rather than altering each page individually).
- A style sheet can act as a template to help different web page authors achieve the same style settings.
- A style sheet makes your pages more accessible to those with visual impairments.

Associating rules with elements

As we mentioned, a style sheet is made up of rules. Each rule applies to certain elements (and usually any elements within that element too). There are two parts to any rule:

The selector indicates which elements the rule applies to. These are written without the angled brackets, so p indicates that a rule should apply to the <p> element.

The declaration indicates how the elements in the selector should be styled.

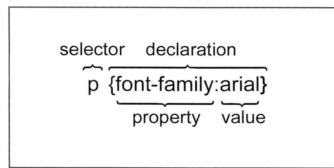

A style sheet rule consists of a selector and a declaration.

The declaration lives inside curly braces and is also split into two parts separated by a colon:

● The property determines which aspect of the element you want to affect (e.g. the colour or typeface used).
● The value specifies the setting for the property (e.g. the colour red or the typeface Arial).

A declaration can be made up of multiple property/value pairs, so you can control several aspects of an element in a single rule. Multiple declarations should be separated by semi-colons (and can be written on the same or different lines). Let's look at a simple example of a CSS rule:

```
p {
    font-family:Arial, Verdana, sans-serif;
    font-weight:bold;
    font-size:12px; }
```

This rule applies to <p> elements, and indicates that the text inside <p> elements should be displayed in an Arial typeface (and if the user doesn't have Arial, then the text should be shown in Verdana, and if they do not have Verdana installed, then the computer's default sans-serif font). It also indicates that the paragraph should be a bold typeface whose size is 12 pixels.

You can also indicate that the declarations apply to more than one element by separating multiple element names with commas. So, if the selector for this example was p, td then these declarations would apply to both <p> and <td> elements.

So, a style sheet is a file that contains one or more of these rules, which govern the overall appearance of web pages. It can be written in a text editor, such as Windows Notepad or TextEdit on a Mac, and should be saved with a .css file extension.

Class and id selectors

CSS allows for some much more complex selectors. There are whole (dull) books dedicated to CSS and we don't have space to go into every aspect of the language here, but there are two special kinds of selector that we should mention:

- Class selectors
- id selectors

Every element that appears in the body of an HTML page can carry an attribute called class and an attribute called id:

- id attributes are used to uniquely identify an element within a document (no two elements in the same document should share the same value for the id attribute).
- Class attributes are used to identify groups of elements. For example, you might want to identify a set of table cells as all being part of a group, such as those that indicate "wins" in a race.

You can use an id selector to identify one individual element and associate a CSS rule just for that element. For example, if you had an element whose id attribute had a value of "mainheadline", you could write a rule that only applies to that one element like this (note that the id selector begins with a # sign):

#mainheadline {font-weight:bold;}

Meanwhile the class selector will apply rules to any elements whose class attribute has a particular value. For example, if several elements had a class attribute whose value was "winner" then you could use a rule like this to indicate those elements should be written in a bold typeface (note that the class selector begins with a full stop):

.winner {font-weight:bold;}

Let's look at a complete example. Here is an HTML table with race winners' details. You can see the simple style sheet that is associated with the HTML page on the right, and the page that you would see in the browser beneath that.

You can use id and class selectors to match elements whose id or class attributes have specific values.

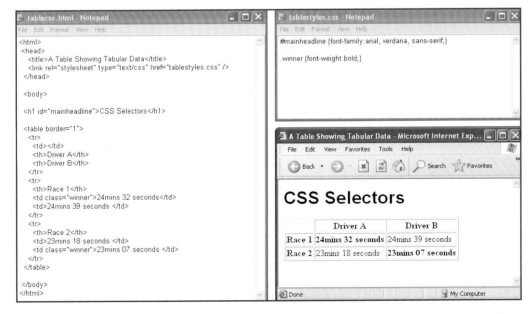

Now that we know how to write a style rule, the question is: what different properties can affect an element, and what possible values can these properties take? We don't have space to cover all the properties in CSS but we will look at some of the most common.

Font properties

If you want to change the typeface that some text is written in, then you can use the following properties. The most common use of these properties would be to specify a typeface you want the page to be written in and its size.

Property	Purpose	Examples
font-family	List of typefaces to be used, in order of preference. Usually this list should end with serif or sans-serif.	font-family:Arial, Verdana, sans-serif;
font-size	Size of font, usually given in pixels (px) or points (pt)	font-size:12px; font-size:12pt;
font-weight	Should font be normal or bold typeface	font-weight: bold;
font-style	Should typeface be italic	font-style:italic

You can also use a shorthand font property that allows you to specify any of these properties in one declaration. For example:

font: 12px bold italic arial, sans-serif;

Examples of controlling presentation of fonts.

You should be aware that designers tend to stick to some of the most common fonts, like Arial, Verdana, Times, Times New Roman, Courier and Helvetica, because a browser will only show the required font if it is installed on the machine. This is why you should specify lists of fonts in case your first choice is not available and cannot be displayed.

When professional designers work on a site, they usually select up to three fonts and stick to just using those. Mixing and matching lots of fonts on the same page tends to look quite amateurish.

Examples of controlling presentation of text.

```
text.html - Notepad
File  Edit  Format  View  Help

<html>
 <head>
   <title>Text properties</title>
   <link rel="stylesheet" type="text/css" href="text.css" />
 </head>

 <body>

 <p id="paragraph1">Some text in paragraph one</p>

 <p id="paragraph2">Some text in paragraph two</p>

 <p id="paragraph3">Some text in paragraph three</p>

 </body>
</html>
```

```
text.css - Notepad
File  Edit  Format  View  Help

p {width:300px; font-weight:bold;}

#paragraph1 {
    color:#ff0000;
    text-align:left;}

#paragraph2 {
    color:#00ff00;
    text-align:right;}

#paragraph3 {
    text-align:justify;}
```

Text properties - Microsoft Internet Explorer
File Edit View Favorites Tools Help
Back · · x ⟳ ⌂ Search Favorites

Some text in paragraph one

                    Some text in paragraph two

Some text in paragraph three

Done   My Computer

Text properties

Here are some properties that allow you to control the appearance of text (beyond which typeface is used):

Property	Purpose	Examples
Color	Change the colour of the text used. Note the American English spelling. We explain how colours are written below.	color:#ffffff; color:#000000; color:ff0000;
text-align	The alignment of text. Values are: left, center, right and justify Note the American English spelling again.	text-align:right; text-align:justify;
vertical-align	The vertical alignment of text. Values are: top, middle, bottom	vertical-align:top; vertical-align: bottom;

The text-align and vertical-align properties are given in relation to the containing element, so a paragraph might be left aligned and a table heading might be centred.

Colours are specified using six-character hexadecimal codes that describe the amount of red, green and blue required to make that colour. 0 means none of that colour and f means the maximum amount of that colour. Here are some examples:

Colour	Hexadecimal code
White	ffffff
Black	000000
Red	ff0000
Green	00ff00
Blue	0000ff

For an extensive reference with 216 different colours and their codes, check out **www.visibone.com/colorlab**. This tool also provides you with a handy reference that helps you choose colours to complement your choices.

Visibone has a handy colour picking tool.

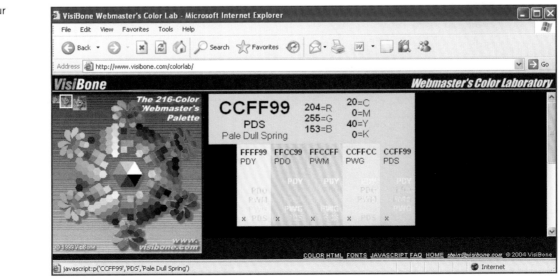

PART 6 **Introducing the box model**

When making your page look attractive using cascading style sheets, it really helps to understand that CSS treats every element as a box (this is known as the CSS box model). You can literally imagine an invisible box being created around every element that lives inside the <body> element of your HTML document.

There are two key types of boxes:

- **Block-level boxes** which are stacked on top of each other. Each new block level box looks like it is on a new line. For example, heading and paragraph elements always appear one above the other.
- **Inline boxes** which can be laid out next to each other without starting on a new line. Examples include the <i> and <b> elements. Obviously enough, you would not want one bold word in a paragraph to have to go on its own line.

Opposite you can see the box model in action, with a border around each box:

The importance of the box model becomes much clearer when you meet the next set of properties, which allow you to control borders, margins and padding.

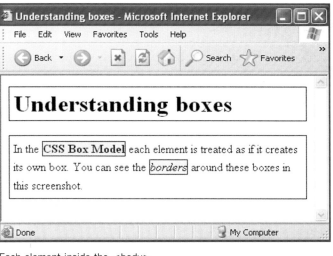

Each element inside the <body> of an HTML document creates an invisible box. Here you can see where the edges of the boxes would be if they were visible.

Borders, margins and padding

As we just explained, you can think of CSS treating each element as if it is in its own box. Each box has three properties: a border that is the edge of the box, a margin that is around the box, and padding that is between the border and the actual element content.

Each box has a border and can have a margin around it and padding inside it.

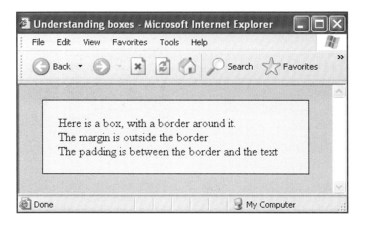

Border properties

By default the border of the box created by an element is invisible. However, you can control the border using these three properties:

Property	Purpose	Examples
border-width	The width of the border, which is usually specified in pixels (px)	border-width: 2px;
border-color	The colour of the border (note the American English spelling of colour). The value should be a hexadecimal colour value	border-color: #ff0000;
border-style	The style of the border. The most common values are solid, dotted and dashed	border-style: solid;

Some examples of borders.

You can specify the border for each side of a box by using properties specific to that side:

border-top-width	border-top-color	border-top-style
border-right-width	border-right-color	border-right-style
border-bottom-width	border-bottom-color	border-bottom-style
border-left-width	border-left-color	border-left-style

You can also use a single shorthand border property, like this:

border: 3px solid #000000;

That gives us a 3-pixel wide solid black border.

Setting margins

You can set the margin *around* any box using the margin property. The size is usually specified in pixels. Margins are particularly helpful when you want to ensure that there is space between elements. For example, if you have text next to an image, then it is a good idea to have some space between the border of the image and the text. This looks professional and makes the text easier to read.

Setting padding

Padding is used when you need space *inside* a box, and is often measured in pixels. It is particularly useful in table cells to make sure that the content of the table cell does not meet the border of the table. This extra space makes it much easier to read the content of the table. For example, this rule indicates that all table cells should have 10 pixels of padding between the border and the content:

th, td {padding:10px;}

Adding padding to table cells makes them easier to read.

Colours of boxes

If you want to control the colour of a box, there are two very handy properties which carry hexadecimal code values (just like the ones we met in the section on font colours):

Property	Purpose	Examples
Color	Controls the foreground colour of a box	color:#ff0000;
Background-color	Controls the background colour of a box	background-color:#efefef;

It is important when choosing colours, and indeed when working on colour schemes for your site, to choose colours that work well together. Perhaps look at design books or other websites for inspiration. You could even look at colour charts that are available from DIY stores. When using combinations of foreground and background colours, you must ensure that there is sufficient contrast to enable to you read any text or see any pictures.

Changing colours of boxes.

Grouping elements using <div> and <span>

Having learned about creating CSS style sheets we should now backtrack and consider two final HTML elements which are particularly useful when working with CSS. Both of these elements are used to group together sets of related HTML elements. This is particularly helpful when you want to apply a style or set of styles to a group of elements. For example, the main links on a site might all use the same style and have a border around them in order to create a navigation bar.

A <div> element is ideal for grouping together elements and applying the same styles to all of them.

- The <div> element creates a block level box, and can therefore be used with elements that create either block level boxes (such as the <p> and <h1> elements, which always start on a new line) and inline boxes (which can appear next to each other).
- The <span> element creates an inline box, and therefore can only be used with elements that create inline boxes (such as the <a>, <img /> and <b> elements).

By way of an example, here you can see a <div> element being used to create a navigation bar for a web page. It is used to create a containing block-level element around a set of <a> elements:

PART ⑥ Creating your first site – using CSS

Having learned how CSS is applied to an HTML document, we should now revisit the example personal site that we built at the end of the section on HTML and transform it using CSS.

Add a link element into the head of the HTML documents so that these documents are associated with the correct stylesheet (mysite.css). It is a good idea to do this before writing the stylesheet so that you can test the stylesheet as you get to work on the HTML document.

```
index.html - Notepad
File  Edit  Format  View  Help
<html>
  <head>
    <title>Tom Smith's Home Page</title>
    <link rel="stylesheet" type="text/css" href="mysite.css" />
  </head>
  <body>

    <h1>Tom Smith's Home Page</h1>
    <p>Home Page | <a href="hobbies.html">My hobbies</a></p>
```

Open a new document in your text editor for the style sheet. Save this file as mysite.css in the same folder as your HTML pages. Then open up the HTML file in a browser next to the CSS style sheet. To see the effect of the changes as you make them, save the CSS file and then reload the page in the browser (Ctrl+R).

To start with, we will add a rule with some properties to control the appearance of the whole of the page. In order for the properties to apply to the whole document, the selector will indicate the body element.

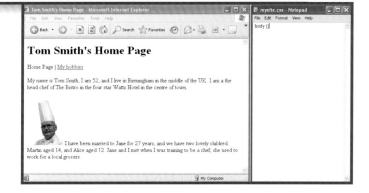

4

Inside this rule, we will add properties to control the colour of the text with the color property and the background colour of the page with the background-color property. We will make the text dark grey using a value of #333333; and a background colour of very light grey using a value of #d6d6d6. We will also ensure that all text in the document appears in one of our preferred typefaces using the font-family property. The first preference of font will be Arial.

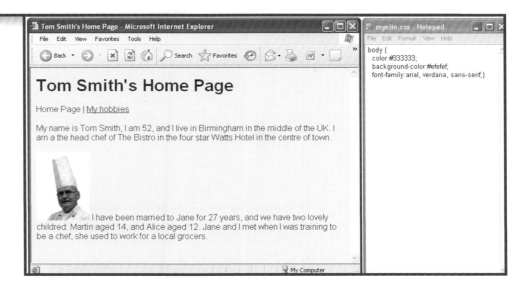

5

Next let's give the level 1 heading a black background and use white text to make it really stand out from the rest of the page. To do this we need to add an h1 selector to the style sheet, and add a color property with a value of #ffffff (white) and a background-color property with a value of #000000 (black).

When there is a visible border to a box, as with the h1 element, it is nice to add padding to create a gap between the edge of the box and the content of the box (in this case, the text).

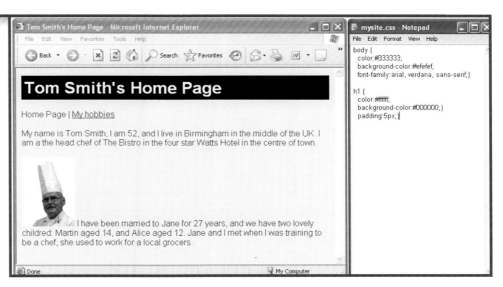

6

In order to control the presentation of the navigation items, we need to add a class attribute to the <p> element in the HTML document. This can be used to distinguish this <p> element from other <p> elements. The class attribute should have a value of "navigation" to indicate that this paragraph of text represents the navigation for the document.

```
index.html - Notepad
File   Edit   Format   View   Help
<html>
  <head>
    <title>Tom Smith's Home Page</title>
    <link rel="stylesheet" type="text/css" href="mysite.css" />
  </head>
  <body>

  <h1>Tom Smith's Home Page</h1>
  <p class="navigation">Home Page | <a href="hobbies.html">My hobbies</a></p>
```

7 –Now that we can uniquely identify the <p> element that acts as navigation, we can use a class selector to apply rules to it. We can set the color of the text to be a light grey using the color property, and the background colour to be red using the background-color property. In order for the background colour of the paragraph to spread across the width of the page, like the background colour of the heading element, you need to add a width attribute with a value of 100%.

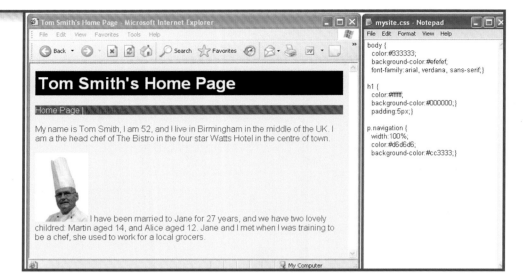

8 To make the navigation slightly easier to read, we should make it bold using the font-weight property. We can also add padding to create some space between the text and the edges of the red box.

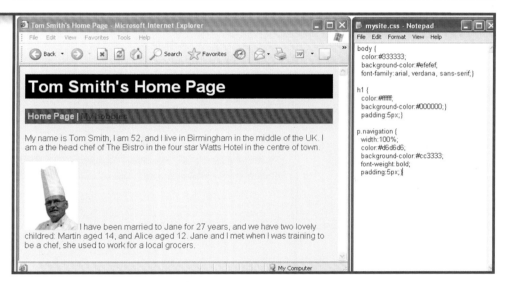

9 To make the link in the navigation fit in a little better with the rest of the page, lets make the text for the link white (rather than the default blue that most browsers use to show links). We just want this rule to apply to links in this navigation bar, so we have to write a slightly more complex selector in the rule, indicating that this rule should only apply to <a> elements that are children of the <p> element whose class attribute has a value of navigation. We have already seen how to select this paragraph using a class selector, and to indicate that we just want <a> elements within this element, we leave a space followed by the name of this element:
p.navigation a {}

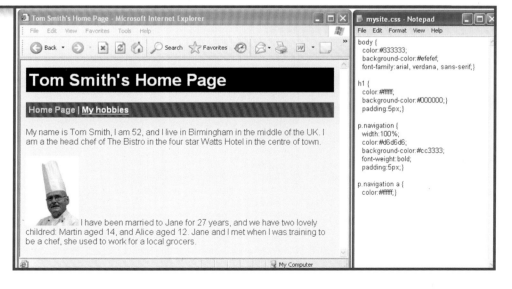

10

Let's add a border around the photo with the border property. We can set the width, style and the colour of the line with just one border property. We should also add a margin around the edge of the photo to prevent the text touching it. This makes the page look better and also easier to read.

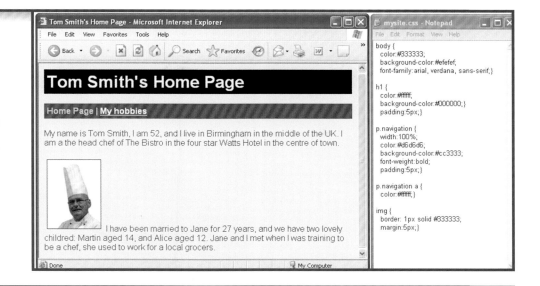

11

There is a gap between the <h1> element and the navigation which it would be nice to remove (bringing these two elements together). In order to do this we need the margin element. If you remember back to the description of the box model, a margin is placed around each box, and by default browsers add a margin around both heading and paragraph elements. In order to remove this margin, we should give the margin property on these two elements a value of 0px.

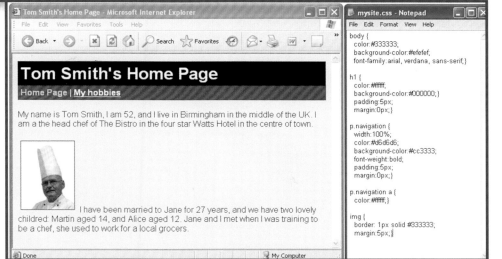

12

Finally, we are going to look at one last property that we have not discussed yet. In order to push the image in the second paragraph of the page across to the right-hand side of the screen, we can add the float property to the properties in the rule that applies to the <img /> element. This float property will have a value of right. While we are at it, we also need to set a width for this "floating" element, as otherwise it will take up the full width of the page. Add a width property with a value of 100px. Done. This simple page now looks a whole lot more attractive, courtesy of a style sheet.

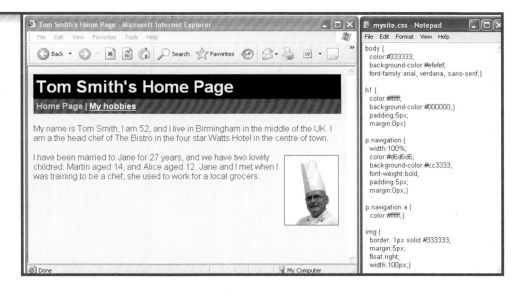

PART **7**

BUILD YOUR OWN WEBSITE

Appendices

PART

Appendix 1 – Search engine optimisation

When you've gone to the trouble of setting up a website you want as many people as possible to visit it, but how do you let them know you're there? Apart from the many incidental ways you can promote your site such as getting it listed in relevant print publications, adding it to your business cards and letterheads, and getting it listed in print and online directories, there are two far more effective methods of attracting visitors:

● Get as many sites a possible to display a link to yours.
● Make sure that your site can be found easily by internet search engines such as Google.

Of the two, the second is by far the most important. Figures suggest that at least 80% of website visitors arrive from a search engine.

How search engines work

If you're going to tweak your website to make it highly visible to internet search engines, you need to know how search engines work. Basically they have three components: a spider (also known as a crawler), a database and an enquiry system. The spider is a program that roams the web examining as many sites as possible. When it visits a site it also follows all the links it finds (these might be to other pages on the same site or to external sites run by other people). The information it finds is stored in the database and indexed. Once a spider thinks it has visited all the sites it can find, it starts all over again looking for changes.

The Yahoo and Google directories are not search engines, they are human-edited and thematically-linked indexes to useful sites. To get your site in the Yahoo directory you pay a fee, but the Google directory is part of the free Open Directory Project and you may suggest your own site for inclusion by visiting **http://dmoz.org/add.html**.

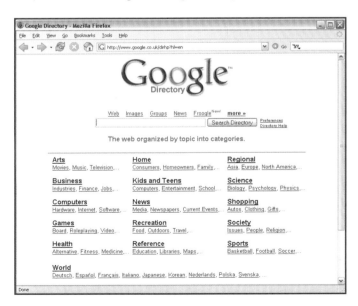

When a user types a phrase into a search engine's enquiry system (which is the only part of a search engine users ever actually see), the phrase is checked not against actual websites but against the indexed database. That's why searches are so fast. It's rather like looking up "plumbers" in *Yellow Pages* instead of reading through the entire book until you get to the page with plumbers on it, which would take weeks.

When a search engine has matched a user's query against its database, it lists the sites it has found in what it considers to be the most significant order: in other words, with the best matches listed first. Search engines often find many thousands of sites matching a particular query so it's crucial that yours should be placed high on the list and preferably on the first page of results. Ideally it will be at the top, but that can be a difficult trick to pull off.

What search engines look for

Every search engine has its own algorithms. Algorithms in this sense are sets of rules that search engines use to decide what's important and what's not. Unfortunately these algorithms are guarded as closely as the secret recipes for Coca Cola or Kentucky Fried Chicken, because the search engine companies know that web designers would use tricks to artificially boost the rankings of their sites if they knew the exact algorithms. But what is absolutely certain, and what is common to all search engines, is that two elements of a site are of overriding importance when deciding rankings: keywords and links.

Each search engine decides for itself which phrases are keywords based on factors such as how close it is to the top of the page, whether it appears in the title, whether it is used as a link and whether you have specifically specified it as a keyword. With a little planning and imagination you can "seed" your web page with phrases that will almost certainly be picked up by most search engines as keywords. The trick is to make sure these keywords are as close as possible to what most users will key into a search engine when they're looking for sites like yours.

To increase the chances of keywords being recognised as such, you should repeat them several times in the body text of each page. Search engines also take account of something called keyword density, which means they look for a high ratio of keywords to ordinary text. Experts reckon that keyword density should be somewhere between 3% and 8% (let's call it 5%), which means that EACH of your keywords should be used 5 times for every hundred words. Bear in mind that search engines concentrate on nouns, verbs and other significant words and do not count so-called stop words which are articles, pronouns, prepositions and other parts of speech.

All the web search engines are in competition for the same users and they're all trying to provide a top-notch service, which means presenting users with sites genuinely relevant to their searches and not directing them to revenue-chasing sites that are padded out with spurious keywords but no real content. Such sites are classified as web spam (as opposed to the more familiar email spam) and they're ignored by search engines. Be sure to play fair with keywords or you could find yourself branded as a web spammer and have your site sidelined or ignored.

Visit the FAQ pages of Google and other major search engines to find out how they analyse web pages, then plan your own site accordingly.

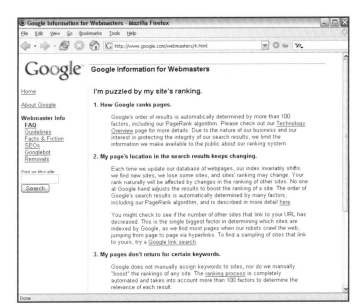

For a list of most of over 500 common stop words visit **www.searchengineworld.com/spy/ stopwords.htm**.

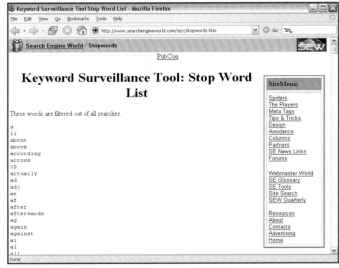

Meta tags and links

Meta tags are special HTML identifying tags that appear in the header section of every web page. The tags' contents don't display on the page but they can be seen by search engines, and although there are quite a few different types the two most important ones are the meta description and meta keywords tags. If you decide to include them (you don't have to), you should place a complete and glowing description of your page after the meta description tag and a list of keywords after the meta keywords tag. Sadly, because these two tags have been so misused in the past by people filling them with screeds of irrelevant and misleading information, most search engines now ignore them. Google doesn't pay attention to either tag, but some rival search engines use one or the other so it's worth including meta tags if you want to cover all the bases.

The way your site uses links is of far more importance to a search engine than whether you've used meta tags. Links between the pages of your site are the way a spider finds its way from the home page to the really meaty parts. Without a well-planned system of internal links, only a fraction of your site might get indexed. Just as important are the links made to your site from external sites. If a large number of sites link to yours, then your site will be regarded as an important one and will be given a better ranking, but not all links are equal: search engines confer a higher ranking on your site if the other sites that link to it are themselves highly ranked. Search engine spiders track links back to their sources and only regard a site as being relevant to yours if it is thematically related and uses similar keywords. If the links all come from the personal websites of friends and family they won't make much impact on your site's status.

You can find relevant sites to link to by typing your site's main keywords into a search engine. You'll discover sites that might be usefully linked to yours and you can then approach them with requests to exchange links. If your site is tailored for e-commerce this is also a way of identifying your competitors. You can't expect competitors to be interested in exchanging links, but once you know who they are you can find out who is linking to their sites, and then ask the same sites to link to yours.

Need more help?

Type "search engine optimisation" into any search engine and you'll find thousands of sites trying to sell you software, books, site design services and marketing tools, but some of the sites do contain genuinely useful free advice, information and interactive resources. One of the best is the webmasters section at Search Engine Watch. Go directly to it by typing **http://searchenginewatch.com/webmasters**. Also worth a look is **www.1hour-search-engine-optimisation.com**, which features a ten-part guide to getting better rankings on search engines. This is extracted from Michael Wong's best-selling e-book on the subject. If it's software you're after, try WebPosition Gold from **www.web-positiongold.com**. The standard version costs $149 so it's not cheap, but there's a 30-day trial version you can play around with.

To learn how many sites link to your site (or any other) simply type link:sitename into Google. There must be no space between the colon and the site's URL, which in this example is **www.haynes.co.uk**.

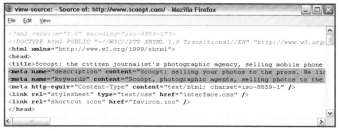

Meta tags for descriptions and keywords should be placed between the <head> and </head> tags at the top of each web page (see p.117).

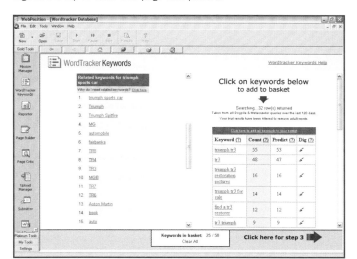

WebPosition Gold is a suite of nine tools to help with search engine optimisation. This screen shows the keyword analysis tool, which not only suggests new keywords but also reports which sites are already using them.

Tips and tricks

The top tip for pushing your site onto the first page of search engines is to get a domain name that embodies your most significant keywords. If all the suitable domains have gone, then put each page in a folder whose name includes suitable keywords. You can see how effective this is if you type "lavender products" into your favourite search engine. When we tried it, eight of the top ten sites listed by Google contained one or both words in their URLs.

- Pick keywords that contain other keywords. For example, if your main business is selling garden tools, use "gardening tools" as one of your key phrases. Search engines can understand compound words so you'll get hits from people searching for both "garden" and "gardening".

- Place the most important keywords in the HTML title tag of every page, and repeat them in the body text close to the top of the page.

- Place keywords in the order users are most likely to type them. Search engines will then judge your page more relevant than others with the same words in random order.

- Use different keywords for each page to reflect the actual content.

- Don't use blocks of graphical text unless there is no alternative. Not only do they slow up the page for people on dial-up connections, but they can't be indexed by search engines. Stick to HTML text wherever possible, and if you must use graphics attach an ALT text description to each one.

- Include as many links as possible (using HTML text not graphics) between the pages on your site. Put them inside the body text and/or at the bottom of each page where both humans and search engines will be able to find them easily.

- Don't attempt to fool search engines by repeating the same keywords hundreds of times, and concealing them by making their text colour the same as the background colour. This is an old trick that every search engine now recognises, and it might lead to the page being rejected as web spam.

- Don't join a link farm, which is an exchange system where hundreds of unrelated sites are cross-linked to each other through pages full of nothing but links. People do this hoping to boost the apparent popularity of their sites but most search engines will see through the ruse and completely ignore the participating sites.

PART 1

Appendix 2 –
An introduction to
e-commerce

The original definition of e-commerce was any form of business transaction conducted electronically instead of on paper, which broadly meant inter-bank and business-to-business transactions such as automated ordering and payment systems. With the easy availability of internet access for all, the latest form of e-commerce involves person-to-person transactions via internet auction sites such as eBay. However, to most of us e-commerce still means only one thing – buying goods and services from online retailers who sell directly to individual consumers.

Shops that never close

Some of the best-known e-commerce companies can also be found in high streets and shopping centres. Tesco is a typical

Watford Electronics, one of the pioneers of mail-order computing in the UK, has reinvented itself as an enormous web-based operation called SavaStore.

Absolutely anything legal (and some things that aren't) can be purchased on the web.

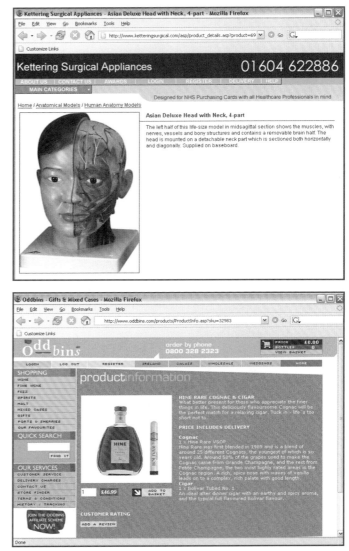

example: it uses the web not only to promote its stores but also as part of a home-delivery operation and as a means of selling specialist items such as wine and financial services at discount prices. In contrast, a great many other companies exist only on the web and depend on it for their survival and business growth. Of these, Amazon is probably the biggest and best known. Even if you've never bought a book or CD from Amazon yourself, the chances are you know somebody who has.

Whether you're interested in setting up a web presence for an existing business or creating an online enterprise from scratch, don't let the technical details put you off: it has never been easier to set up an e-commerce site. Just be sure that before you take the plunge and put up a live site, you've already sorted out the "back-end" of the business, including having sufficient stock to meet demand, plus a well-organised packaging and delivery operation.

Web shop essentials
Established companies use networked computers to perform administrative and financial functions. Part of the arrangement is usually a structured database system storing details of goods, prices, suppliers and the current stock situation. To add web sales to a system like this is no simple matter. Typically, you need specialist software to link the network to a dedicated internet server, and expert help will be required to implement and maintain both hardware and software. The result will be a fully integrated system that not only provides an internet shop window for the company's products but also passes details of web transactions to the existing order system for processing.

At the other extreme, you can set up a new small enterprise using a rented web shop to sell your goods. Whenever an item is sold, you're informed by email and it's up to you to process the order in any way you see fit. There is no connection between the web shop and your own PC or network. In theory, you could even run this type of business without a PC by using a mobile phone to receive email notifications.

In between the two extremes are dozens of web trading systems involving varying degrees of complexity, but what they all have in common is the identical experience they provide to customers. Potential buyers are able to search or browse for products of interest, and having found a product they can store it in a temporary electronic "basket" while they continue to shop. There is a checkout system where purchases are totalled and carriage charges are added, and there are forms for the collection of personal information such as names and delivery addresses. Finally, of course, there must be a secure means of accepting electronic payments by credit or debit card.

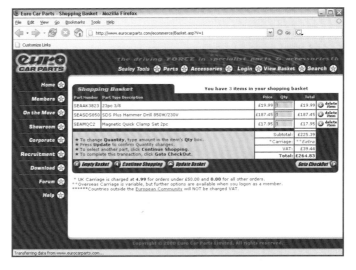

Impulse purchases and last-minute gifts are the stock-in-trade of many web stores.

Whether it's called a shopping basket or shopping cart, it's where goods are held until a customer is ready to check out and pay.

The simplest solution

For start-up businesses with no pre-existing company website, the simplest and cheapest way of getting into e-commerce is to rent an e-shop that can be configured and set up using only a web browser. The resulting web pages do not reside on your computer at all, but on the computers of the company renting you the shop. When sales are made and payment has been received (usually through PayPal or WorldPay), you receive a notification by email. The cost of renting a web shop varies according to a number of factors, but principally it's the number of different products you wish to sell, the amount of web space you'll need and the level of traffic you expect to handle. Charges range from £10 to £60 a month. At the lower end of the scale you may be restricted to selling only a handful of products, while at the upper end you're allowed hundreds of products and will be able to set up a searchable product catalogue complete with photographs and descriptions.

One of the disadvantages of a web shop maintained solely through a web browser is that you don't get a chance to customise your site other than in ways provided by the host. This makes it difficult to give your shop site a unique look and feel, and it means you have no base for further development if you decide you've outgrown your existing site. On the other hand you can operate your site from literally any computer with an internet connection.

More advanced web shops

A step up from the simplest browser-driven web shop is one where you construct your site with the help of design templates and software wizards. The finished shop is translated into HTML code, which you are allowed to modify to a certain extent by changing elements such as headers and footers, and by adding scripts. A script is a fragment of code you can paste into the HTML at specific points to customise various elements. You pay a monthly rental which covers the shop's design tools and the cost of hosting it on a fast internet server. Financial transactions are usually limited to PayPal, but sites like these can easily be upgraded if your business grows.

Most shop hosts offer a tiered pricing system where for a small extra payment you can sell more products and use more pictures on your site, and you'll be given greater freedom to add personal touches. If you pay the very top rate, you'll get a web shop that can be fully customised and completely integrated with your company's main website. Other benefits include being able to download transactions and customer data in a form suitable for using with your database or spreadsheet program, and there is no restriction on the number of products in your catalogue. You might also be covered by a shared secure site certificate enabling you to accept confidential information such as credit card numbers from your customers. Most web shop providers (regardless of the service level chosen) are able to provide comprehensive site traffic reports and help with getting your shop listed on internet search engines.

A fully-functional website constructed and maintained using only a web browser, available from **www.doyourownsite.co.uk**.

At 1&1 Internet (**www.1and1.co.uk**) you can buy literally any internet service, including upgradeable web shops.

The bespoke option

Hand-made e-commerce sites come in all shapes and sizes. If you're already running a successful website and you understand the basics of HTML coding you can graft a simple shopping cart system onto your existing site and this will enable you to take customer orders and link to PayPal for payment processing. It won't cost you anything to implement and there'll be no monthly charges other than what you're already paying for web hosting.

Although bespoke sites are a cheap option for those with the ability to create their own, serious business users are not drawn to them for this reason. For them, site design is usually sub-contracted to a professional designer who will produce an eye-catching site that works as it should and is fully secure. Larger organisations might even employ a full-time web wizard, and host their e-commerce facility on the company's own server instead of through a hosting service, especially if e-commerce transactions are to be linked to the company's existing order processing system.

The advantages of a bespoke site are that you can:

- seamlessly integrate your company's e-commerce and offline trading operations;
- set-up an e-commerce site that accurately reflects your company's corporate identity;
- customise the contents of your site for different countries and currencies;
- enjoy total flexibility to offer the services you think your customers need, rather than the ones built into a web shop template;
- process payments from virtually any source.

Custom-designed sites like Amazon's can generate extra trade by making recommendations based on past purchases.

When selling essentials, the simplest approach is sometimes the best: make it easy for customers to find exactly what they want and they'll come back time and again.

Handling money online

E-commerce could not exist without safe ways of making payments online. There are several ways of going about this and the method that's right for you will depend on the nature and volume of your business, and on whether you already have a merchant account with your bank that allows you to take credit cards.

If you don't have such an account, perhaps because you are just starting up, the simplest and most convenient systems are those run by payment bureaux such Nochex (**www.nochex.com**), PayPal (**www.paypal.com**) and WorldPay (**www.worldpay.com**). Once you've established an account with one of these companies, you will be provided with the necessary software to link your e-commerce system to the payment bureau's own site. When your customers check out the contents of their shopping baskets on your site they are transferred to the payment bureau's site where they enter their credit or debit card details. Once payment has been received, you are notified by the payment bureau and can then process the sale. Almost anybody can open a service bureau account provided they have a current bank account and a credit card. Charges are generally calculated per transaction and may be as high as 4.5%. Though this seems steep, there are no set-up costs and no subscriptions or service fees to pay, so if you make no sales in a particular period you pay no fees. This makes a payment bureau the ideal system for start-up and micro businesses, which is why many of the entry-level web shops incorporate them as the only option for processing online payments.

Established businesses with merchant accounts at their banks and who are already equipped with a swipe machine for point-of-sale credit card transactions can upgrade their merchant account to accept "customer not present" transactions. This allows customers to phone, fax or send their credit card details for manual processing, but its too labour-intensive if you anticipate handling a significant volume of online sales. It's far better to ask your bank if it will add Internet Merchant Services (IMS) to your merchant account. If it will, the only other thing you need is a Payment Service Provider (PSP) to handle individual transactions on your behalf. In effect, a PSP acts in place of a swipe machine by collecting customer details over the internet and passing them to your bank for authorisation.

Although it sounds complicated and expensive to operate an e-commerce site using a merchant account, it can actually work out cheaper despite having to pay set-up, fixed charges and commissions to both your bank and your PSP. It all depends on whether you expect to maintain a sufficiently high volume of transactions. Another benefit is that banks perform stringent checks before authorising a customer for IMS, so the very fact you're not using a payment bureau gives your business instant credibility.

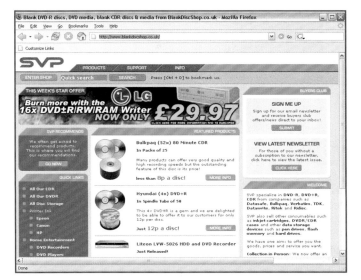

SVP sells optical discs and related items through a bespoke website at **www.blankdiscshop.co.uk**. Its thousands of satisfied customers all pay their bills through uncomplicated payment bureaux.

At 2.6p + 20p per transaction, Nochex is probably the cheapest way to handle payments up to £100, but PayPal and WorldPay are better for larger amounts and international transactions.

Index

Acknowledgments:
Grateful thanks to Jon Duckett,
Gary Marshall and Paul Wardley

Author	**Kyle MacRae**
Copy Editor	**Shena Deuchars**
Page build	**James Robertson**
Index	**Nigel d'Auvergne**
Project Manager	**Louise McIntyre**